NEXT STOP: *Joy*

DEDICATION

This book is dedicated to my grandma, Charlotte. Your life and love were an example of what it means to live for Christ. I'll meet you at the gate.

NEXT STOP: *Joy*

©2025 Nancy Garrison Ministries
All rights reserved. No portion of this book may be reproduced or shared in any form - electronic, printed, photocopied, recording, or by any information storage or retrieval system, without prior written permission from the publisher. The use of short quotations is permitted.

ISBN - 978-1-952840-75-3

Unless otherwise noted, Scripture quotations are taken from THE HOLY BIBLE, NEW LIVING TRANSLATION® Copyright © 1996, 2004, 2015 by Tyndale House Foundation. Used by permission of Tyndale House Publishers, Inc., Carol Stream, Illinois 60188. All rights reserved.

UNITED HOUSE Publishing Clarkston, Michigan
info@unitedhousepublishing.com www.unitedhousepublishing.com
Author Photographs: Seth Snider; sethsniderphotography.com
Interior Design: Talitha McGuinness; talitha@unitedhousepublishing.com
Printed in the United States of America 2025 - First Edition

SPECIAL SALES:
Most UNITED HOUSE books are available at special quantity discounts when purchased in bulk by corporations, organizations, and special interest groups. For more information, please email orders@unitedhousepublishing.com.

A 30-Day Journey To A Life
Overflowing With Godly Joy

NEXT STOP:
joy

Nancy Garrison

Foreword by Gwen Smith

NEXT STOP: Joy

NEXT STOP: *Joy*

FOREWORD
by Gwen Smith

When our kids were itty-bitty, my husband Brad and I used to hold little hands a lot. Sometimes it was to protect them from danger. Sometimes it was to calm fears or to help them feel secure. Sometimes it was because we were on a mission to get through or to a place quickly. Other times it was for the simple pleasure of strolling, skipping, and smiling together.

Now that they're adults, my kids aren't so keen on holding hands with Mom and Dad anymore. And I miss it. I love locking fingers with my people. There's beauty and intimacy to it. A tangible connection that binds our skin and braids our souls. I love walking with them, hearing their hearts, talking through tight spots, giving advice, gaining wisdom, laughing, and enjoying their company.

Similarly, our heavenly Father finds pleasure when you and I walk with Him; when we take His hand and share our time, trials, treasures, and thoughts. The prophet Micah spoke to this. "He has shown you, O mortal, what is good. And what does the Lord require of you? To act justly and to love mercy and to walk humbly with your God" (Micah 6:8). This is a simple, yet profound summary of God's desire for us. A revealing of His longing for you and me to live in constant communion with Him. To lace our fingers with His in good, bad, scary, and sad times. Whether the sun is high in the sky or thunder rumbles low in our hearts. Whether joy comes easily or we have to fight for it.

NEXT STOP: *Joy*

I long for God to consider me a woman who walks faithfully with Him. I long for the Lord to see me as one who reflects his strength, dignity, and love. One who embodies and exudes His radiant joy. Yet, as much as I long for these honorable notions to all be true, it could only be by grace, as I am, sadly, often found walking in my own independence and self-reliance. Ugh.

I don't want to be the girl who only reaches for God's hand when the road is bumpy, when my checkbook is empty, or when my feet are stumbly. And I don't want to be like the teenager who's embarrassed by her dad and only gives him attention in private or on occasion. I want to live with the faith of a child who acts justly and loves mercy. As a mature woman who is totally tethered to the joy of Jesus and daily takes the hand of her Father to face each moment, mountain, and memory right by His side.

Each of these writings by Nancy Garrison has pointed my heart to the goodness of God and to the plan of joy He has for my life through the work of the Holy Spirit in me. They've nudged me beyond numbing failures and flounderings to the freedom found in Christ. The devotions are funnels of relatable fun that have led me to God's heart with Scripture and stories and have placed my hand in His to walk closer with Him each day.

This devotional you're holding contains a lifetime of learning. Nancy shares her wins and her losses. From her failures, fears, and funnies. She vulnerably opens up her life on these pages to help you walk with joy and victory in yours. To help you walk hand and hand with Jesus. As believers, we're encouraged to spur one another on in faith. To sharpen one another as iron sharpens iron. To meet each other in dark spaces of the night and help each other fight for and find places of grace and light. These writings do just that.

As you read, expect Nancy to be a new girlfriend who will be present with you in the trenches of truthing and trusting.

NEXT STOP: Joy

The kind of friend who will laugh with you, cry with you, stay with you, listen to you, and cheer you on – sometimes all in the same devotion! All because she knows firsthand the importance of yielding heart, mind, and soul to the leading and kneading of the Spirit of God, who has sealed and grafted the life of every believer to eternal life in the love and finished work of Jesus.

What resonates most in the words of this devotional is the power joy has to change a life. It bludgeons bitterness, softens our sorrows, and grapples with our grumpies. It whittles away weakness, anger, resentment, and hard-heartedness, while it ushers in strength, peace, forgiveness, grace, and light-heartedness. It's my prayer that this devotional will affect you in similarly powerful and personal ways.

Gwen Smith
Author, Speaker, Worship Leader,
Owner of AMADA Senior Care Charlotte,
Host of the Graceologie with Gwen Smith Podcast
www.gwensmith.net

NEXT STOP: *Joy*

"There's Supposed To Be WHAT Down In My Heart?"
Introduction

I'm so excited you have begun the journey of intentionally filling the joy deficit in your life. I want you to know "joy" does not come easily to me. This book is a result of a journey God has led me through to craft joy into my own life. I wasn't even aware of the void of joy in my life until God brought it to my attention.

It all began on a late December evening. My daughters were home from college; it was my favorite time of the year. I LOVE CHRISTMAS! I love decorating, gift-giving, baking . . . all of it! But mostly, I love having my family together. We were attempting to have "family movie night," but my anxiety was so animated that instead of enjoying the movie, I was struggling not to have a complete and total breakdown. I said I was tired and needed to go to bed. But the truth was, I just couldn't hold it together for one more minute. So, instead of being with my family, I found myself alone, sitting in my bathroom, sobbing uncontrollably. I was absolutely miserable and lower than I could ever remember being in my life. I then heard an audible voice I had never heard before whisper in my ear, "Nancy, you know there is enough medication in this bathroom that would allow you to escape this misery forever." Now I wasn't just depressed and anxious, but terrified!

In complete and utter desperation, I called out to God, "Please don't leave me here!" I uttered this request out loud over and over again. I must have prayed that prayer over 100 times that night. I texted a friend of our family and asked him to pray for me because I knew I was under a spiritual attack. Eventually, I was overcome with exhaustion and went to bed. Life appeared to be "normal" for the next few days.

It was a little less than a week later, New Year's Eve. I was on vacation in the mountains with family and friends, trying to put on a happy face and pretend to enjoy the trip. While alone in my room, getting some rest before we went out to dinner to celebrate the new year, I received a text message from a pastor friend. He told me that while he had been praying that morning, he had felt God telling him a couple of things to share with me. He then asked me if I had been under any spiritual attack. I told him, "Absolutely! Possibly the worst I had ever experienced in my life."

He had me call him right away. He first shared with me, "God wants you to know that He's not going to leave you where you are." ARE YOU KIDDING ME?! I immediately began to cry. That had been my prayer in my darkest hour. God had heard me! He SEES me! And then my friend shared that God wanted me to know I had been finding my worth in things other than Him. I wasn't overly surprised to hear that (more on that later).

Not finding my worth in God significantly contributed to my eventual state of despair. I was blessed to be a stay-at-home mom when my daughters were young. As they grew, I was able to work at their schools and be an active part of their day-to-day lives. There was nothing I enjoyed more than being their mom. As they left for college and my nest emptied, I felt lost and struggled to find any purpose for my life. But I had it all wrong! I needed to find my value as a child of God and a daughter of the King. So, I began a journey to discover how to live the way God had called me.

The next day was New Year's Day 2022. I prayed and asked God to give me a word to aid me in my quest to find my worth in Him. I heard an audible voice again, but this time it was from God. He said, "JOY is your word." I actually laughed out loud. I felt like Sarah, Abraham's wife, when she heard that she would have a baby at the age of ninety. I thought, "That's hilarious! I don't even really know what joy is!"

I waited a couple of days and asked God again. He said, "Joy!"

So I answered, "OK, if this is going to be my word, then I will need You to show me what that means and how to craft it into my life."

For the next two months, I was bombarded with the word "JOY." It appeared in podcasts I was listening to, devotionals I read, sermons, and songs—even in casual conversations. Joy was popping up everywhere in my life, so much so that I started writing down everything God was showing me. My life truly began to change. For the first time in my fifty-four years on this earth, I was authentically experiencing a joy-filled life. Not a perfect life, not a life free from stress or frustrations, but a life rooted in the joy that can only come from the God who created it. I felt like I had been healed. Upon reflection, I realized God had shown me exactly thirty truths. Twenty-five ways to cultivate godly joy, and five things I've identified as "joy busters"—things that will rob you of authentic joy.

I pray you find new applications and wisdom each day as you seek to fill your joy deficit. I look forward to sharing with you all that God has taught me. Every day will provide an opportunity to dig deeper into a specific aspect of joy, answer some thought-provoking questions, and journal what God reveals to you personally. I expect a "joy revival" in your life, family, and community.

Love, Nancy

NEXT STOP: *Joy*

Day 1
All-Access Pass

"Do not be afraid, I bring you good news that will cause great joy for all the people."
Luke 2:10, NLT

Most of us didn't start at the top of our careers. Do you remember your first mundane, bottom-of-the-corporate-ladder job?

I personally spent two long, traumatic weeks in the fast food industry.

If you've ever been unfortunate enough to work the night shift at an entry-level position, you know an extra layer of dullness occurs as time passes through the dead of the night.

The shepherds, who were the first ones to be notified of Jesus' birth, were working a very difficult, twenty-four-hour-a-day, seven-day-a-week manual labor job.

Imagine being half-awake, walking through the paces of your evening tasks, when the angel, Gabriel, in all of his splendor and brilliance, appears before you out of nowhere.

The shepherds must have jumped right out of their sandals. I can almost imagine them rubbing their eyes, shaking their heads, and staring at each other with a "are you seeing what

I'm seeing?" expression on their faces.

Gabriel knew his glorious presence would be overwhelming, so he began the encounter with, "Do not be afraid . . . "

He then announces the good news that the Messiah has been born and tells the shepherds that His birth will bring "great joy."

Not just a little joy or some pretty-okay-joy, but *GREAT* joy!

Even better than that, this great joy would be for *everyone*.

The angel alerted them that God, in human form, had arrived on earth and that Jesus' birth was about to change everything.

The Bible reveals that Jesus came to save, heal, and rescue mankind. He was the bridge that would make God accessible to us.

2 Corinthians 5:21 says, "For God made Christ who never sinned, to be the offering for our sin, so that we could be made right with God through Christ." *That's definitely cause for great joy!*

We all have a degree of longing for something eternal — a relationship with our Creator. Jesus paved the way for that. When He came to earth and was eventually crucified, He took on our sins. His sacrifice gave us the atoned-for opportunity to come into God's presence and be forgiven for our wrongs.

This would follow Gabriel's proclamation of that sleepy, seemingly average night. The only path to authentic, God-fueled joy is through Jesus. There's no shortcut, no GPS alternative route. All roads point to Him.

Joy depends on who Jesus is, rather than who we are or our circumstances.

NEXT STOP: *Joy*

Real joy is crafted into the truth that we are saved, forgiven, and reconciled with God.

What would you do if I gave you the winning lottery ticket for the next big jackpot? Having the winning ticket in your possession wouldn't be enough for you to take home the millions of lottery dollars. You would have to cash it in for it to have tangible value.

If we hear the news about Jesus but never act upon it, it's like having the winning lottery ticket but not claiming the prize.

If you have never experienced the great joy of receiving Jesus into your heart, I encourage you to consider it today.

If you're a Christian, you already have an all-access pass to the great joy the angel announced in the fields on that pivotal night.

Over the next few weeks, we will explore ways to bring that joy to the forefront of our daily lives.

Jesus, thank you for coming to earth to be my Savior and for dying on the cross for me so I could be forgiven and set free from sin. I want Your joy—the true, authentic, life-giving joy You alone can give. Open my heart and mind to receive all You have for me through this journey. Amen.

Questions for Reflection:
1. How would you define joy?

2. How would you describe the "good news" the angel revealed to the shepherds? (Luke 2:10)

NEXT STOP: Joy

3. Why might that create great joy for all humanity?

Journal Prompt
How has having direct access to God impacted you? Describe a time when communicating with God made a difference in your life.

Day 2
Right Over Left, Then Under

"Don't look out only for your own interest, but take an interest in others, too."
Philippians 2:4, NLT

As a little girl, I remember being in awe of my grandma's domestic talents. She seemed just to *know* how to do stuff.

She could grow, cook, or create almost anything. She used to hand-decorate all of our birthday cakes, grow all kinds of homegrown vegetables, and at one point, maintained a thriving boutique of handmade, custom geese clothes to fit the trendy concrete lawn decorations of the early 2000s.

And while I know she took great pride in her abilities, she was always ready and willing to share her secrets.

One day, I was especially intrigued by how she tied the belt on her coat. I asked her how she was able to make the fastening so perfect. She said it was called a square knot. She then grabbed some ribbon, put it around my waist, and walked me through the steps. "Right over left, then under. Left over right, then under. Pull it tight, and there you go." She had dozens of glowing attributes, but most of all, I remember she was generous, especially with her talents, love, and attention.

NEXT STOP: Joy

Has your life ever been impacted due to someone's loving generosity? The very first thing God taught me about joy was that it can't exist without generosity. And not just polite hospitality, but I had to learn to be authentically generous. So, I started eagerly sharing attention, smiles, kindness, patience, and grace. I let people in front of me when merging on the highway, even if they didn't use their turn signal.

I let my husband add mushrooms to our pizza order (Well, on half of the pizza, but still). As I lived out this narrative, something began to change inside me. Instead of being consumed with my despair and problems, I focused more on others.

Jesus told a parable in Luke 10:30-37 that details precisely what generosity should look like. You've probably heard the story of the good Samaritan many times. A man was traveling from Jerusalem to Jericho when he happened upon a wounded man who had been left for dead on the side of the road. Instead of avoiding him like the others who had passed by earlier in the day, the Samaritan went over to the beaten man, clothed him, loaded him up, and took him to a hotel. We don't know where the Samaritan was headed, but he wasn't on this treacherous road for a scenic hike. He gave the wounded man his time and attention, knowing that it would inconvenience him and change the course of his day.

He was generous with his resources when he poured oil and wine on the man's wounds and bandaged them.
The Samaritan put his own needs aside when he placed the man on his donkey and continued the journey on foot. He then invested in the man's future by offering to cover any debt he accrued at the inn.

There is absolutely no connection between these two men except that they ended up at the same place at the same time while taking separate journeys. Yet, the Samaritan displayed generosity in every way imaginable to a total stranger.

NEXT STOP: *Joy*

God perfectly outlines generosity for us in John 3:16: "For this is how God loved the world: He gave His one and only Son, so that everyone who believes in Him will not perish but have eternal life." He held nothing back. Just like the good Samaritan, He gave us everything, knowing we had no way to reciprocate.

When I prioritized generosity in my life, my problems and struggles didn't magically disappear, but something remarkable did happen.

A healing began within me.

Joy started peeking its way into my heart and daily life. It then began to multiply the more I made others a higher priority than myself. If you want a joy-saturated life, make intentional generosity your daily goal.

Dear Heavenly Father, thank you for giving me the most generous gift of all when You sent Your Son to die for me. Help me to honor You by living a life overflowing with generosity. Make me aware of when and how I can give to others. Open my eyes and heart to see people the way you see them. Nudge me when I become distracted and self-absorbed. Amen.

Questions for Reflection:
1. Which part of the parable of the good Samaritan stands out to you the most (Luke 10:30-37)? Why?

2. Where in your life can you be more generous?

3. In what ways can you intentionally live with more generosity?

Journal Prompt:
Write about a time when you either observed or displayed great generosity. How did that lead to joy?

Day 3
It's Not About You

"Do nothing out of selfish ambition or vain conceit, but in humility consider others better than yourself."
Philippians 2:3, NLT

I spent most of my childhood in a small town surrounded by a large extended family.

My older brother and I were blessed to spend almost as much time at our grandparents' house as we did our own.

Bring on the spoiling!

It was the best!

Grandma was the picture-perfect stay-at-home mom, and Grandpa was a hard-working, blue-collar World War II veteran *(Imagine Marion Cunningham married to Archie Bunker)*.

There were countless memories made on road trips, nights sitting on the back porch, and meals at the little kitchen table.

I should've been living my best life, but instead, I wasted an immense amount of energy brooding over a lie I allowed to roam free in my head.

NEXT STOP: Joy

Have you ever missed the best part of something because you allowed your inner voice to distract you?

Grandpa had always wanted a son, so his relationship with my brother was extra special. Somehow, that translated into my brain as, *I'm not good enough. I'm not important.*

I allowed this fabrication to grow louder and louder until I was convinced it was true. I carried it around with me everywhere I went. I could feel its weight in every aspect of my life, especially my relationships with people and God.

It wasn't until my late twenties, and after some God-led counseling, that I was able to see how that distortion was damaging my life and my connection with my Heavenly Father.

I'd been ignoring God and who He said I was.

I'd been struggling all of those years because I made something all about me that really didn't have anything to do with me.

I could see that Grandpa was so excited about his grandson because it filled a large void in his life. He was only two years old when his dad was killed in a coal mining accident. My brother provided the father-son relationship that he never had.

God showed me clearly that my misconception was a barrier keeping me from experiencing true joy.

The older brother in the parable of the prodigal son (Luke 15:11-32) had a very similar problem.

Usually, when you hear this story, the focus is on the younger son and his lessons of grace and redemption. But the older son is a perfect example of how "making things all about you" can rob you of joy.

While everyone was partying and celebrating the younger brother's return, he was outside pouting and refusing to join in the excitement. *"The older brother became angry and refused to go in. So his father went out and pleaded with him. But he answered his father, 'Look! All these years I've been slaving for you and never disobeyed your orders. Yet you never gave me even a young goat so I could celebrate with my friends'"* (Luke 15:28-29).

The oldest son couldn't experience the elation of having his brother return home because he was too busy thinking about himself.

It's impossible to experience joy while living this type of self-centered life. This is one of Satan's most effective tricks. It clouds our perspective and wastes our energy. If he can keep us consumed with worrying about who we aren't, we will completely miss who God is telling us we are.

So, how do we turn off this destructive way of thinking?

Start by asking God to show you where destructive thought patterns have taken hold in your life. If you find yourself holding a grudge or being hyper-critical of people, there's a good chance you're making something about yourself.

Ask God for clarity and healing from this thought pattern.

Living firmly anchored in God's truth will inevitably lead to increased joy.

All-Knowing Heavenly Father, thank you for understanding me better than I understand myself. I'm sorry for the time I've wasted on my self-centered thinking. Please show me if there's any area of my life where I have the older-brother mentality. Reveal any displeasing lies I'm holding on to. I ask for healing and clarity, in Jesus' name. Amen.

Questions for Reflection:
1. In the parable of the prodigal son, how would you describe the older brother's perspective of the party being

NEXT STOP: Joy

thrown for his younger sibling (Luke 15:11-32)?

2. How did that rob him of joy?

3. Why does "making something about you that's not about you" hinder a healthy relationship with God?

Journal Prompt:
When have you made something about you that wasn't really about you? What's a new, godly, truth-filled way of looking at that situation?

___

___

___

___

___

___

___

___

___

Day 4
I'd Been Waiting for This

"For everyone has sinned; we all fall short of God's glorious standard. Yet God, in His grace, freely makes us right in His sight. He did this through Christ Jesus when He freed us from the penalty for our sins."
Romans 3:23-24, NLT

One of my favorite life quotes is, "I give grace because I've received grace." That means we should offer it to others because God so generously gifted it to us.

That sure sounds a whole lot easier than it is.

A few years ago, my willingness to live out this motto was put to the ultimate test. Several months after her breakup from a long-term relationship, I found out my daughter's boyfriend had been abusive. Needless to say, I was heartbroken and enraged.

A year later, I was shocked to hear from him. He had made amends with her, but he wanted the opportunity to meet with me to apologize and take responsibility for his actions.

I'd been waiting for this.

I was looking forward to telling him exactly what I thought of him.

NEXT STOP: Joy

Have you ever been so mad at someone that you rehearsed all the mean things you wanted to say to them?

I was fully prepared to let him have it!

But something unexpected happened when he opened the door and got into my car. I felt the overwhelming presence of the Holy Spirit wash over me, reminding me of all the things I'd been forgiven of.

A true miracle happened as the young man sat in my car crying and asking for my forgiveness. Instead of unleashing my fury on him, I could talk about God's grace and feel compassion.

Examples of godly grace can be found throughout the Bible.

Paul's conversion is one of the most dramatic, grace-fueled stories. Before he became a follower of Christ, Paul was known by the name "Saul." As Saul, he made it his life's work to find, arrest, and execute anyone who believed that Jesus was the Messiah.

Saul was traveling to Damascus, the capital of Syria, to carry out this very mission when he encountered God's grace head-on.

He was going about his business when he was completely blinded out of nowhere. He fell to the ground on the dirt road when he heard an audible voice say, "Saul, Saul, why are you persecuting me?"

Shaken, Saul replied, "Who are you, Lord?"

The shocking response was, "I am Jesus, the one you are persecuting" (Acts 9:6)! From then on, he was called "Paul," and his new mission was to share the gospel and plant churches.

Paul explained it best in a letter to his friend Timothy: "The grace of our Lord overflowed for me with the faith and love that are in Christ Jesus" (1 Timothy 1:14).

Obviously, Paul didn't get what was coming to him. He was hunting down and torturing God's children. But in place of receiving an arguably just punishment, he received forgiveness. Paul definitely acknowledged that he had done wrong, and he changed the way he lived. But forgiveness and restoration—that all started with grace.

God did not offer that gift just to Paul; it is available to each and every one of us.

Joy is found in knowing we are covered in God's grace. Our mistakes don't define us and imprison us.

We didn't do anything to deserve the pardon, but God loves us and desires a relationship with us.

That alone is reason to be joyful.

But there's more . . . *overwhelming* joy results when we then extend the same grace to others.

Not because they deserve it, but because we didn't either.

Heavenly Father, thank you so very much for the beautiful gift of grace. Thank you for sending your son, Jesus, as a sacrifice so we can be fully forgiven of our sins. Please show me where I'm not letting Your grace into my life and where I might be withholding it from others. Amen.

Questions for Reflection:

1. What do you think of when you hear the word "grace"?

2. What part of Paul's conversion stands out most? (Read Acts 9)

NEXT STOP: Joy

3. How might experiencing and extending grace lead to joy?

Journal Prompt:
Describe a time when you've experienced God's grace. When have you extended it to someone else? Is there an area of your life in which you haven't been able to show grace? Why?

Day 5
The Coveted Golden Ticket

"For wherever there is jealousy and selfish ambition, there you will find disorder and evil of every kind."
James 3:16, NLT

I learned a great deal about myself when my oldest daughter was in high school, playing on a competitive travel volleyball team and attempting to earn one of the coveted golden tickets to a Division I college scholarship.

The once low-growling dog of comparison, which had been a strong deceiver in my life, began to bark ferociously in my ear as I came face-to-face with my deep insecurities. The financial demands were a struggle for our family, and trying to keep up with what everyone else was doing became a howling lie of inferiority.

In hindsight, I can see where I took my eyes off God and bought into the comparison game of getting more attention, training, and accolades.

Where in your life does that dog bark the loudest?

We've been learning ways to cultivate joy in our lives up until now. Today (and every fifth day of this journey), we will identify a "joy blocker."

NEXT STOP: Joy

It's exactly what it sounds like—a joy blocker is a barrier to experiencing God's authentic joy.

Comparison is one of the most common obstacles. It can lead to jealousy, frustration, and resentment.

We'll know when we're in its grasp if we find ourselves either: 1) tearing other people down to make ourselves look better, or 2) convincing ourselves that we are "less than" because we don't measure up to our perception of others.

Shamefully, I admit I allowed myself to be led down the path of envy, gossip, and bitterness. I bought into the fabrication that other people's successes or failures were a measuring stick of my worth.

I lost sight of God and the value He placed on me (and my daughter). The story of two sisters, Leah and Rachel, is a shining example of how destructive comparison can be (Genesis 29:15-35; 30:1-24).

Both sisters were consumed with envy because they were comparing themselves to each other.

The story begins with Jacob falling deeply in love with Rachel and asking her father for her hand in marriage.

Rachel's father tricks Jacob into marrying his less desirable eldest daughter, Leah. Rachel is jealous of Leah because she is very fertile, while Rachel is desperate to have children but remains barren.

On the other hand, Leah is consumed by the knowledge that her sister is Jacob's first choice.

Both women became increasingly bitter, believing they weren't as good as the other.

This is where we can easily get tripped up.

NEXT STOP: Joy

It wasn't Leah and Rachel's circumstances that robbed them of joy; it was their misconception that their identities were defined by anything other than God. Rachel found her identity in whether or not she could have a child; Leah found hers in being desired by her husband.

There's nothing wrong with wanting either of those things. The problem was that they saw them as qualifications of their worth.

Comparison is a joy blocker that God called me out on pretty early in my joy journey. When I took a step back, I was quite surprised to see how it dominated my thoughts. I was convinced I wasn't smart enough, pretty enough, or gifted enough.

Comparison blocks us from joy because it springs from the belief that what God has given us isn't enough. We believe the lie that our lives would be better if we gained what others have.

Join me today in flipping the script by asking God to block any narrative of comparison we allow in our lives.

Dear Heavenly Father, forgive me for the moments when I have found my self-worth in anything other than you. You are my creator, and You alone define who I am. Please clarify any areas of my life where I'm allowing comparison to have a stronghold and quiet the enemy whose lies would lead to confusion and discontentment.

Questions for Reflection:
1. How did comparison affect the relationship between Rachel and Leah? (Genesis 29:15-35; 30:1-24)

2. How do comparisons show up in your life?

NEXT STOP: Joy

3. How might comparison block us from joy?

Journal Prompt:
Describe a time when you let comparison get the best of you. What were some negative results of that? How could you handle the situation differently if faced with it again?

Day 6
A Prickly Pear

For God has not given us a spirit of fear and timidity, but of power, love and self-discipline.
2 Timothy 1:7, NLT

I know the word "self-control" can be triggering; however, this isn't going to be a list of rules born from the roots of legalism but a deeper look into the last characteristic listed in Galatians 5:22-23.

Paul tells us self-control is one of the fruits of the Spirit. Although for me, it has always felt more like a prickly pear than a scrumptious, delicious apple. How about you?

I had no idea how little of this fruit was being produced in my life until I took on the challenge of writing this book. After finishing a few chapters, I was stuck and unable to move forward.

I spent a lot of time in prayer trying to get "out of the mud." God showed me several areas in my life that needed improvement before I could move forward. So, I started consciously practicing obedience in everything, no matter how insignificant it seemed.

I needed to change some habits, ask for forgiveness from some people, and settle some debts. After speaking with a trusted mentor, I concluded that God was teaching me discipline and self-control.

Those are great Christ-like characteristics to strive for, but what do they realistically look like, and why are they so important?

The assumption would be that "self-control" is simply the ability to control oneself. But that's just stating the obvious.

It's an authentic transformation in our character, a result of the Holy Spirit's work within us. In actuality, self-control really means Holy Spirit-led discipline. We weren't reconciled with God on our own. It was through Jesus' sacrifice for our sins, so it makes sense that we can't grow as Christians on our own. We need guidance from the Holy Spirit.

Philippians 2:13 tells us, "For God is working in you, giving you the desire and the power to do what pleases Him."

Self-control and discipline aren't negative, taking-away-my-freedom, governing directives. They are God lovingly giving us a solid defense when tempted to sin.

In ancient times, a city built a strong wall around its perimeter to prevent enemy forces from attacking.

There were people of authority stationed at guarded gates who decided who was safe to let in and who should remain outside. They essentially served as community bouncers.

That's what self-control is for us. It's a protector that frees us from becoming enslaved to the instant gratifications of this world that are almost always a pathway to sin.

We can actively strengthen our protective defenses by being disciplined to have community with other believers, spending time reading and studying the Bible, and having a thriving prayer life.

NEXT STOP: Joy

There is a direct line from self-control and discipline to joy, as it brings us closer to the life God intended for us—a life free from sin and its consequences.

I have learned that this is a journey, not a destination. It's a daily focus and priority. If discipline and self-control are challenging to you, start by practicing them in small areas of your life. I was so pleasantly surprised to see how God blessed even the smallest act of obedience.

God, thank you for loving me the same in both my failures and triumphs.. Please give me a desire for discipline and self-control, not to bring attention to me but to be more in Your will. Show me the areas in my life that lack these fruits and guide me to obedience.

Questions for Reflection:
1. Why do you think self-control is included among the fruits of the Spirit? (Galatians 5:22-23)

2. How could living a disciplined life lead to joy?

3. Where do you feel God is telling you you need more self-control?

NEXT STOP: Joy

Journal Prompt:
Write about a time in your life when a lack of discipline or self-control negatively affected you. How can God use it to grow you?

Day 7
Menopause-Fueled Hot Flashes

And give thanks for everything to God the Father in the name of our Lord Jesus Christ.
Ephesians 5:20, NLT

One of the best ways to achieve a joy-filled life is to adopt an "attitude of gratitude."

It might sound a little corny, but stay with me . . .
It's more than just remembering to say "thank you" or feeling delighted by a gift you receive; it's genuine, unconditional, God-fueled gratitude.

1 Thessalonians 5:18 instructs us to "be thankful in all circumstances for this is God's will for you who belong to Christ Jesus."

All circumstances? Really?

So, God wanted me to be thankful when my husband lost his job? When my loved one was diagnosed with a scary illness? Or when I couldn't get a good night's sleep because of menopause-fueled hot flashes?

The short answer is "yes." The scripture says "*in all circumstances*," but this doesn't come naturally for most of us.

NEXT STOP: Joy

When have you struggled to feel gratitude?

If we truly desire to live out this scripture, the first thing we have to do is change our focus. This year for Christmas, I bought my three-year-old nephew a pair of binoculars. When he first started using them, he kept looking through the large end, causing everything to appear to be farther away instead of closer.

All he had to do was turn them around to get the desired results.

That's exactly what we do when we focus on our circumstances instead of God's goodness. We're looking through the wrong lens.

Jesus modeled this for us on the day He fed thousands of people with only a few loaves of bread and a couple of fish.

It's not only one of Jesus's first miracles, but it's the only one in His ministry recounted in all four gospels. This implies that it had a profound impact on everyone who was there that day.

A very large crowd had formed to hear Jesus speak. The Bible records that there were 5000 men plus women and children (John 6:8-10).

This story is often used as a reminder to trust God to meet our needs, which is awesome, but if we're not careful, we can overlook Jesus's example of godly gratitude.

Obviously, Jesus knew there would be enough for everyone to eat, and a dozen baskets full of leftovers would remain.

When the disciple Andrew presented Jesus with only five loaves of barley bread and two small fish to share with the masses, Jesus first thanked God before breaking the bread and performing the miracle (v. 11).

He didn't give thanks because He thought there was enough food, but because He knew God was enough.

I don't know about you, but when I find myself overwhelmed by life's circumstances or faced with unmet needs, my first response isn't usually to give thanks. But that's exactly what we can and should do.

It's easier to do than you might think. It's just a matter of shifting focus. Instead of honing in on what's in front of or around us, we all need to look up and trust that God is who He says He is.

If we focus on God, living a life of gratitude becomes easier. Joy will be a bonus byproduct of our thankful life.

Almighty God, thank you for Your unfailing love and goodness, even when I forget to acknowledge it. Forgive me for taking my eyes off You and allowing my life to become overwhelmed with fear and worry. Change my perspective so I can see all things through a lens of gratitude. Alter my heart and my thoughts to mirror the change. Amen.

Questions for Reflection:
1. What does living a life of gratitude look like to you?

2. What are you most thankful for? Where is it difficult in your life to feel grateful?

3. Read John 6:1-15. Why do you think He paused and gave thanks first?

Journal Prompt:

Write a letter of gratitude to God. Ask for His help in areas where you are struggling to be thankful.

Day 8
Riding the Struggle Bus

"But let all who take refuge in You, rejoice; let them sing joyful praises forever. Spread your protection over them, that all who love Your name may be filled with joy."
Psalm 5:11, NLT

Today, I feel like I'm riding the struggle bus to find joy. I woke up with an overwhelming feeling of melancholy.

Absolutely nothing has changed in my life overnight. I'm in the same house and living the life I was thankful for yesterday.

Maybe it's the dreary January sky as I'm writing this, but I have a big ole case of the blahs. As I fight the internal battle of whether or not I want to get up and get going or just snuggle in deeper and continue to scroll on my phone, I'm reminded I indeed have a choice.

You've probably heard the phrase "joy is a choice." Although it may seem a bit clichéd, it's a necessary reminder because that's precisely what differentiates it from happiness. Happiness is an emotion we feel as a result of our circumstances.

I'm most happy when I'm reclining on a cushy lounge chair, feeling the sun's warmth, and digging deep into a plate of poolside-delivered nachos. (I'm smiling just thinking about it.)

But joy is not determined by what we're currently experiencing.

It's a powerful option, not a feeling.

As women of God, we not only have a direct line to the Joy-giver but also get the opportunity to model intentionality in living our authentic, joy-filled lives. That doesn't mean putting on a fake smile, posting a filtered selfie, and pretending to have a perfect existence.

We have to be genuine.

Life is tough! Every one of us goes through heartache, loss, and injustice to some degree. The world we live in is far from perfect and always will be.

However, we are confident in our choice of joy because we look to God, not our situation, as a guide.

It's not always easy; there's no app for that.

It's born from consistently leaning into God, rather than our surroundings and feelings. Does that mean we can have joy even when we're lonely, scared, or exhausted? You bet it does!

David, the author of Psalm 13, models this beautifully. He begins his writing in utter despair, "O Lord, how long will You forget me? Forever? How long will you look the other way" (v 1)?

No matter how strong you are in your faith, there has likely been a time when you felt like God had just completely forgotten about you. David clearly felt alone and totally abandoned. Many scholars believe he wrote this during a time when King Saul was trying to kill him (1 Samuel 12:1-2). Running and attempting to hide from a powerful king who had the resources of an entire nation at his disposal had to make David feel overwhelmed, helpless, and frightened.

NEXT STOP: Joy

But keep reading . . . by the end of the Psalm, David has shifted his focus back to God and remembered His goodness: "But I trust in your unfailing love. I will rejoice because you have rescued me. I will sing to the Lord because He is good to me" (v 5-6). What a total 180.

Nothing changed about David's circumstances from verse one to verse six, but he turned his eyes back toward God and remembered His character. When he fixed his gaze upon his Heavenly Father, David was able to choose joy because he knew he could trust in God and His faithfulness.

The same is true for you and me. On days when we feel downhearted, abandoned, alone, or forgotten, we can still choose to trust God and find joy in His unfailing love.

Dear Heavenly Father, thank you for being patient with me when I get overwhelmed by my circumstances instead of Your goodness. I'm sorry for the times I choose to focus on fear or worry instead of joy. Please continue to remind me of your never-ending goodness. I put my trust in you! Amen

Questions for Reflection:
1. How would you describe the difference between joy and happiness?

2. When is it most difficult for you to choose joy?

3. Read Psalm 13. What are the two verbs David uses in Psalm 13:5? How can you apply those to your above response?

NEXT STOP: Joy

Journal Prompt:
Think of a time when you felt like God had forgotten you. Rewrite Psalm 13 in your own words, reflecting on that situation.

Day 9
The Cheat Code

"The Lord is my Shepherd, I have all that I need."
Psalm 23:1, NLT

When I was a little girl, I used to pretend to have long, beautiful, flowing hair. I would often put a towel around my head, stand in front of my mirror with my hairbrush microphone, and pretend to be my favorite star, Cher.

On Sunday evenings, I would sit mesmerized in front of the TV as Cher majestically shook her gorgeous mane from side to side until she reached the crescendo of the now-infamous hair flip.

But my reality couldn't be further from my beauty icon.

No matter what I did, my heavily textured hair would never grow longer than the top of my shoulders.

It's always been a lot of work, and I've always hated it. I coveted long locks so much that I cried tears when my youngest daughter cut hers to a stylish bob. (Sidenote: She looked adorable.) As I've matured, I've learned to accept and appreciate what God has given me. I've embraced my natural curls (*most days*) and allowed them to live in their beautiful state of chaos.

Ironically, almost once a week, someone tells me they wish they had my curly hair. Isn't that just like us women? We always think that we would be happier or more content if only we had _____ (fill in your blank).

Being content in life is not a natural state for most of us. I'm much better at complaining than I am at being satisfied. God has recently taught me that these two things can't coexist.

It's either one or the other.

But how do we find contentment in a world constantly telling us we're not good enough, don't have enough, and are falling behind?

Paul does a great job of answering that in Philippians 4:11-13 (NLT):

"Not that I was ever in need, for I have learned how to be content with whatever I have. I know how to live on almost nothing or with everything. I have learned the secret of living in every situation, whether it is with a full stomach or empty, with plenty or little. For I can do everything through Christ, who gives me strength."

Paul is giving us the cheat code, and he should know. He experienced extreme levels of suffering as one of the most persecuted leaders of the early church.

He wrote these words on contentment while serving time in prison for sharing the gospel.

Paul tells us that contentment must be learned and is not tied to our circumstances.

That doesn't mean we can't have desires or work towards making positive life changes. It means that we look only to Jesus to fulfill us.

If we attempt to find peace and satisfaction in anything other than Him, we will ultimately end up right back where we started. *Everything* else will fall short. Through Jesus, we can live a contented life even during tough times, even when we're disappointed, and even with curly hair.

Joy is found in the truth that He will always be enough, in control, and the source of our strength.

All we have to do is trust Him, believe He loves us, and give us the strength to endure all that life may throw our way.

Dear Jesus, thank you for being all that I need! Please show me when I'm complaining or grumbling instead of being content with what You have provided. I will be joyful because You alone are my strength. I praise you! I trust you! I love you! Amen.

Questions for Reflection:
1. How would you define contentment?

2. Where in your life do you struggle with feeling content?

3. Why can Paul be as content with nothing as he is with everything (Philippians 4:11-13)? How can being content lead to joy?

NEXT STOP: Joy

Journal Prompt:
What are some things you thought would make you happy but didn't? Write a letter to your younger self, offering her advice on how to find contentment in Jesus.

Day 10
Caught in the Act

"This means that anyone who belongs to Christ has become a new person. The old life is gone; a new life has begun!"
2 Corinthians 5:17, NLT

Divorce? Never in a million years would I have expected that.

But one night, just a few months after our second wedding anniversary, my husband told me he no longer wanted to be married.

I was in shock. I didn't see it coming. Sure, we had disagreements and conflicts, but divorce wasn't an option (or so I thought).

How could this be happening? I had followed the formula. After high school, I attended a Christian university and met a man who checked all the boxes. The truth eventually came out as everything unraveled over the next few weeks. He'd been having an affair.

He had no interest in saving our marriage and insisted I move out. I returned to my parents' house and began the long process of healing and rebuilding my life. My first time going to church after moving back home was rough.

I can still feel the overwhelming shame and humiliation

of walking into the sanctuary again. Just a couple of years earlier, I had stood at that very altar and spoken my vows in front of a church full of our family and friends.

I felt like *"failure"* and *"disgrace"* were written all over me.

I felt exposed, vulnerable, and broken.

Shame can be a significant barrier to joy. It's impossible for the two to co-exist.

The woman caught in the act of adultery and dragged before Jesus while He was teaching must have felt the same way (John 8:1-11).

As a woman, I'm struck by how terrifying it would have been to be grabbed by a group of men and physically forced into the public courtyard. The Bible doesn't say what she was wearing, but it does say she was "caught in the act" (v.4). I imagine she was most likely in some state of immodesty. I can almost feel her skin burning with embarrassment as she stood there, desperately trying to cover herself and listening to them describe what she had been doing.

The bigger picture was how the Pharisees attempted to trick Jesus into saying something against the law and using it against Him. However, I'm sure it did absolutely nothing to lessen her trauma and humiliation.

Jesus proceeded to remind them that they had all sinned and were being hypocritical. They ended up leaving one by one. The woman was then abandoned by her accusers and alone in front of Jesus.

I'm so thankful her story doesn't end here.

Without verses ten and eleven, we would've logically assumed she had slipped away and lived her life in disgrace.

But that's not where Jesus left it.

Instead, He speaks directly to her. He tells her He doesn't condemn her, and to go and live a changed life.

Jesus knew that just letting her escape punishment wasn't enough. He also freed her from the shame and condemnation of her sins.

Shame has never been part of God's plan for us.

We undoubtedly have all experienced our share of missteps. We have all sinned and had to confess our brokenness. The Bible assures us that God hears and forgives us.

"But if we confess our sins to Him, He is faithful and just to forgive us our sins and to cleanse us from all wickedness."
1 John 1:9, NLT

We can't accept forgiveness and continue to live in shame.

Once our sins are forgiven, they're gone. Psalm 103:12 says, "He has removed our sins as far as the east is from the west."

I'm not great with directions, but even I know that's about as far away as it gets. If we allow shame to live in our identity, it will choke the joy out of our lives. If we want joy to blossom in and through us, we must pull out and discard any shame we've allowed to take root. Jesus alone can heal the wounds left behind.

I'll never be happy about being a divorced woman. But it's no longer a source of shame for me. It's just part of my story. God has even allowed me to use it to comfort and encourage many other women who have had similar struggles.

Godly joy grows when we exchange our hurts and shame for love and healing.

Dear Jesus, thank you for forgiving me of my sins! Help me to live in the truth that You have removed them as far as the east is from the west. I want to live the shame-free life that You have for me. Remove anything I'm holding on to that keeps me from experiencing Your joy. Amen.

Questions for Reflection:
1. How would you describe what shame feels like?

2. Read 2 Corinthians 5:17. What are the two things that are new through Christ? How does this make it possible to let go of shame?

3. How can shame be a hindrance to joy?

Journal Prompt:
Think of a time when you experienced shame. How does God's response to shame differ from the world's?

_____

_____

_____

_____

_____

_____

_____

Day 11
Team God

"When all the people of Israel saw the fire coming down and the glorious presence of the Lord filling the Temple, they fell face down on the ground and worshiped and praised the Lord, saying, 'He is good! His faithful love endures forever!'"
2 Corinthians 5:17, NLT

I *love* the college football season!

I especially love the tradition, the rivalries, and the tailgating.

I was born and raised in Ohio, so I'm a diehard Ohio State Buckeye fan. As much as I enjoy watching the games on our big flat-screen TV, there's nothing quite like experiencing it live at the Ohio Stadium, nestled snugly beside the Olentangy River in Columbus.

Before the game even starts, the energy from the parking deck is already palpable. The chants begin in the tunnel as fans march toward their shared destination. The atmosphere is one of expectancy and unity as the pack of over 100,000 individuals joins together for their shared goal of cheering on their team. Once inside the stadium, the intensity of the fans' roar is a force like no other. Half the enormous crowd answers "*I-O*" as the other half calls out, *"O-H."* We all lose any sense of awareness and dignity as we get lost in the competition taking place on the field.

During a crucial moment for the team, one of the players raises their arms to encourage the fans to take the roar to an even higher level. The team has already done everything necessary before kickoff to prepare for the game. Workouts have been endured, film has been watched, practices have been executed, and game plans have been set.

The players' and coaches' talent and skill exist regardless of whether the fans are present. But the team will collectively take on new energy as they absorb the love and adoration of their home crowd.

What if we approached praise and worship of our God with the same passion? What if we enthusiastically proclaimed our love and adoration of our Lord and Savior, Jesus Christ, with the same unbridled joy and celebration we do for the winning touchdown?

Imagine if we put on our metaphorical "Team God" jersey, applied our face paint, and shook our pom poms while we shouted Psalm 95:1-7:

Psalm 95

1 Come, let us sing to the Lord! Let us shout joyfully to the Rock of our salvation.
2 Let us come to him with thanksgiving.
Let us sing psalms of praise to him.
3 For the Lord is a great God,
a great King above all gods.
4 He holds in his hands the depths of the earth
and the mightiest mountains.
5 The sea belongs to him, for he made it.
His hands formed the dry land, too.
6 Come, let us worship and bow down.

NEXT STOP: *Joy*

Let us kneel before the Lord our maker,
7 for he is our God.
We are the people he watches over,
the flock under his care.

Much like the gifted athletes, God doesn't require us to acknowledge Him in order for Him to be great. But our praise and worship of Him is a selfless act of love that connects us to God.

We worship God because of all He's done for us, to bless and honor Him, and to keep our hearts focused on Him. But one of my personal favorites is because it draws us into His presence. Oh, what great joy exists in worshiping God and being with Him through the gift of His Holy Spirit.

Almighty God, thank you for the beautiful gift of worship and for sending the Holy Spirit to allow us to experience Your presence. My heart overflows with praise at the thought of even a moment with You. Remind me of my priorities and to stay intentionally connected to You. Amen.

Questions for Reflection:
1. Read Psalm 95 above, circle all the descriptions the psalmist declares about God.

2. Why do you think it's important to make time for worship?

3. What are some of your favorite ways to worship God?

NEXT STOP: Joy

Journal Prompt:
Write a declaration of praise to God, describing who He is to you.

Day 12
Ride or Die

"So encourage each other and build each other up, just as you are already doing"
1 Thessalonians 5:11, NLT

My all-time favorite movie is *The Breakfast Club*. John Hughes wrote, directed, and produced the 1985 film, which tells the story of five teenagers from different high school cliques who serve Saturday detention together.

At the beginning of the film, the brain, the athlete, the basket case, the criminal, the princess, and the jock had nothing in common. But by the end of detention, they had bared their souls and become comrades.

They passed the long hours by dancing together, revealing their secrets, and opening up about their struggles. They discovered they weren't really that different after all.

They all had experienced genuine hurts and failures. And they ended up empathizing and relating to each other.

I identified deeply with the outcast, Allison. I remember crying tears in the movie theater as she confessed how she'd been hurt. When asked what the people she loved in her life had done to her, her tearful reply was, "They ignore me."

Yes! That's it! Me too, Allison!

I don't know if I'd ever felt more understood than at that very moment. It still chokes me up every time I rewatch it.

Cue: Simple Minds singing, "Don't You (Forget About Me)"

Due to restructuring at my dad's company, my family moved frequently. By the time I graduated, I'd been the new girl at three different high schools. I spent the majority of my teenage years feeling lonely, unknown, and disconnected. I didn't have childhood friends that I'd grown up with or classmates with shared nostalgia.

Like the characters in the movie, I yearned for an inner circle that understood me and would share my struggles with me.

Haven't we all had times when we were the girl going through life feeling conspicuously unattached? Whether it's a new school, job, relationship status, or community, being the outsider looking in is a deep kind of loneliness.

It's uncomfortable because it goes against how God created us. We aren't meant to go through life isolated and alone. Jesus modeled this by choosing a group of friends to accompany Him as He traveled and preached the gospel.

One of my favorite examples of friendship in the Bible is found in Luke 5:18-25. A large crowd had gathered at a home where Jesus was staying. Four men showed up carrying their paralyzed friend, but they couldn't even get close to Jesus because of the large group of people already there.

Instead of trying to fight their way or just giving up and going home, these crazy guys climbed on top of the roof and lowered their friend down on a mat through the tiles into the middle of the crowd, right in front of Jesus.

NEXT STOP: *Joy*

Jesus praised the faithfulness of him and his friends. Verse 20 says, "Seeing their faith, Jesus said to the man, 'Young man, your sins are forgiven.' And then Jesus tells him, "Stand up, pick up your mat, and go home!"

Talk about your "ride or dies!"

We'll all experience times when life paralyzes us. This pain could be physical, mental, emotional, or spiritual. But there is joy in having a friend (or four) to help lead you to Jesus for healing.

Likewise, there is great joy in being one of the individuals who lifts the friend to the Savior.

Like the students in *The Breakfast Club*, we must allow ourselves to be vulnerable, share our struggles, and support one another.

Isolation and alienation aren't God's desire for us. We can't "bear one another's burdens and truly hurt along with those hurting" (Galatians 6:2) if we never spend any time together to find out what those burdens and hurts actually are.

Heavenly Father, thank you so much for creating us to be in community. Please help me cultivate a desire to connect with other women. I want to protect and deepen my current relationships while also becoming more aware of others around me who may feel isolated and alone. I want to be the type of friend who will cut a hole in the ceiling to show my girlfriends more of You. Amen.

Questions for Reflection:
1. Read Luke 5:18-25. Jesus is the Healer and Savior, but what role did friendship play in the miracle of the paralyzed man?

2. How big of a role do friendships play in your life?

3. What can you do to make sure having and being a good friend are part of your godly priorities?

Journal Prompt:
Write about a time when someone was a great friend to you and walked alongside you in your struggle. (Or maybe you were the good friend lowering someone through the roof.)

Day 13
Sitting on the Dock of the Bay

"Now may the Lord of peace Himself give you His peace at all times and in every situation. The Lord be with you all."
2 Thessalonians 3:16, NLT

Everyone wants peace, but few people have it. However, if joy is our destination, then peace is one of the necessary pit stops on our journey. Living a peace-filled life is a work in progress for me. I lean more towards anxiety and dread than peacefulness.

I'm also easily annoyed and struggle to tolerate being uncomfortable. In our home, I usually control the thermostat, the remote, and the Spotify playlists. *My husband is a saint.*

When I reflect on a time in my life when I felt the most peaceful, I'm taken back to a vivid memory of a Saturday morning when I was a little girl.

Before cell phone alarms existed, my parents had a clock radio on their nightstand that played music to wake them up. It was exactly like the one that roused Bill Murray's character in the movie *Groundhog Day* morning after morning to the sounds of Sonny and Cher singing "I've Got You Babe."

NEXT STOP: Joy

On this particular day, instead of jumping up, grabbing a bowl of cereal, and turning on my favorite cartoons like I did at the start of most weekends, I remember lying quietly in my bed, feeling the rays of sunshine warming up my room and taking in the familiar noise of my dad singing along with his clock radio.

I've always loved hearing my dad sing, but that morning, hearing him croon a duet with Otis Redding to the lyrics of "Sitting On The Dock Of The Bay" personified peace to me. I focused on nothing but the familiar, comforting sound of my father's voice.

When was the last time you felt at peace, fully satisfied, all-is-right-with-the-world peacefulness? Maybe you've never experienced it, but have always longed for it. Perhaps, like me, you struggle to keep it.

The story of Mary and Martha in Luke 10:38-42 makes me think of what peace should look like. These sisters and their brother were some of Jesus' closest friends. He spent some of His last days on earth in their home.

It can be assumed that they were a wealthy family who could afford to accommodate and feed the large crowd accompanying Jesus. They were followers of Him and believed He was the Messiah. Martha appeared to be the head of the household and very much in charge. This account shared that on this particular day, "Martha was distracted by the big dinner she was preparing" (v 40).

If you've ever hosted a dinner party, you can imagine what it would've been like to expect such a large number of guests, let alone the Son of Man, coming over for the evening meal. I can almost see Martha fluttering around anxiously, trying to make everything as appealing as possible before the group arrives.

Martha gets irritated with her sister because instead of helping her, "Mary sat at the Lord's feet, listening to what He taught" (v 39).

NEXT STOP: Joy

Mary is so at peace in the Lord's presence and listening to Him that she ignores many of the day's traditions. Mary sitting at the feet of Jesus might seem like a touching and sweet picture to us. But in first-century Jewish customs, this would have been shocking. A woman wouldn't have been allowed to receive formal biblical teaching, be in close and intimate physical proximity to a rabbi, or be seated amongst a group of men.

But Mary completely ignored these cultural limitations. Instead, she chose to do two specific things: first, she "sat at the Lord's feet," which was an act of submission. Then, she "listened to what He taught," which showed a desire to learn from Him.

I think it's safe to conclude that we can, too, find peace in our lives by mirroring Mary's actions. Are we submissively listening to Jesus so intently that we block out the stress and distractions of the world? Or is it the other way around?

When I was little, the sound of my dad's singing brought me such peace because it connected me to the person who made me feel safe and loved. Peace will certainly follow if we remain closely attuned to Jesus and actively seek His voice.

Dear Jesus, You alone are the source of my peace. Your word teaches me that You are the Prince of Peace. Please give me a submissive heart and a desire to learn from Your Word. Today I want to sit at Your feet and allow You to be my single-minded focus. Amen.

Questions for Reflection:
1. Describe how it feels to be peaceful.

2. Read the story of Mary and Martha (Luke 10:38-42). What did Mary prioritize over her domestic duties?

3. How does spending time with Jesus and His Word lead us to a peaceful life?

Journal Prompt:
Write about a time in your life when you felt at peace. Write about the story of Mary and Martha from Mary's perspective. How might she have described it?

Day 14
Who Needs the Famous Mouse?

"Jesus Christ is the same yesterday, today, and forever."
Hebrews 13:8, NLT

For a kid in southern Ohio, nothing was better than spending a day at Kings Island, a 364-acre amusement park near Cincinnati.

Kings Island was so popular in the 1970s that episodes of *The Brady Bunch* and *The Partridge Family* were filmed there.

Does it get any cooler than that?

Who needs the famous mouse? We had Marsha Brady. The park is renowned for setting records with its innovative and often thrilling roller coasters. And on a hot day in the summer of 1980, the country's first forward and backward looping coaster tested my bravery.

I was usually the kid standing on my tiptoes to be tall enough to ride the big rides. I loved the anticipation, the thrill, the adrenaline rush . . . all of it! And as soon as it was over, I couldn't wait to do it again. But the Screamin' Demon (the name says it all) had me shaken.

The line for the ride consisted of climbing five stories and 150 steps. As the potential riders ascended the mountainous stairs, they watched as the people above them were sent screaming through a 54-foot-tall loop (caught their breath) and then were catapulted *backwards* through the same loop.

I was just shy of my thirteenth birthday when I finally passed the qualifying mark to be considered tall enough to ride. According to the little line on the wooden measuring post, I was no longer in danger of falling out.

I was ecstatic!

It never occurred to me to question how they arrived at that conclusion. I didn't consider the educational background of the physicists who made the calculations or what formula they used.

Without a second thought, I trusted the mark, the bars holding me in my seat, and the teenager who closed the harness around me. Even though the anticipation of being suspended upside down was terrifying, I believed the mechanics of the giant steel loop were completely reliable.

What if we trusted God's character with the same conviction and assuredness? What if we believed God still had us firmly in His grip even when life throws us through loop after loop?

Unlike the qualifications of the engineers who designed the Screamin' Demon, we do know God's qualities. We don't have to guess or make assumptions. The Bible gives us clear insight into God's attributes.

God is one of a kind, unique, and without peers. It would be impossible for us to fully understand who God is, but by knowing some things about Him, we can live a joy-filled life in His unchanging truths.

- God is omnipotent—all-powerful. Jeremiah 32:17 (NLT) states, "O Sovereign Lord! You made the heavens and earth by Your strong hand and powerful arms. Nothing is too hard for you!" Is there any greater comfort than knowing there is not one thing we will encounter in life bigger than God?

- God is omniscient. Psalm 147:5 (NLT) tells us, "How great is our Lord! His power is absolute! His understanding is beyond comprehension!" In other words, He knows everything, including us. We all want to be known. I have spent much of my life feeling like no one understands me. The Bible assures me God does.

- God is omnipresent, meaning He is everywhere at all times. In my introduction, I mentioned being at my lowest and calling out to God, pleading not to leave me in my brokenness. Although I felt so encased in darkness, I knew God was there, even if I couldn't see or feel Him. Psalm 139:7-10 (NLT) declares, "I can never escape from Your Spirit! I can never get away from Your presence! If I go up to heaven, You are there; if I go down to the grave, You are there. If I ride the wings of the morning and dwell by the farthest oceans, even there Your hand will guide me, and Your strength will support me."

We're all going to face times in our lives when we feel like we're being propelled through unseen twists and turns. Some will be minor inconveniences, and others will send us screaming and grasping to hang on. We can find joy even then; even though we may not be able to see what's over the next hill, we know that God does, and He will be there with us, capable of holding us firmly through the entire ride.

Dear Heavenly Father, thank You for who You are. I rest firmly in the truth that Your character does not change. I may not be able to grasp all that it means fully, but I put my faith in the knowledge that You are all-powerful, present, and all-knowing. You're never taken by surprise. You're with me even through my most challenging times. Amen.

Questions for Reflection:
1. Which characteristic of God is the most difficult for you

NEXT STOP: Joy

to comprehend and why?

2. How does knowing God never changes bring you joy?

3. Rewrite one of the Bible passages from above that you will stand on when life throws you for a loop.

Journal Prompt:
Write about one of the "biggest roller coaster rides" you have experienced. How does knowing God's characteristics make it less scary?

Day 15
My Golden Calf

"Jesus replied, 'You must love the Lord your God with all your heart, all your soul, and all your mind'."
Matthew 22:37, NLT

Prior to my thirtieth birthday, I was adamant that I never wanted to be a mom. To be quite honest, I found kids and babies annoying. Unlike most of my friends, I hated babysitting as a teenager. And except for my nephews and niece, I had zero desire to interact with children in any way.

I was convinced God just hadn't given me any maternal instincts (Not to mention the thought of a mini person taking over my body, and then finding a passageway out, terrified me).

But seemingly out of nowhere, something changed drastically in me when I hit that third decade of my life. It was almost like a switch had been flipped. I was suddenly hyper-aware that my life needed to be about something more than me.

My husband and I were blessed to welcome our beautiful daughter just months after our first wedding anniversary. And two years later, our family was completed with another healthy, happy, amazing little girl.

NEXT STOP: *Joy*

I couldn't believe how much I loved being a mom. It gave me a sense of purpose and belonging that I had never experienced before. Raising these tiny humans into thriving adults had become my top priority. Don't get me wrong, I made plenty of mistakes and had to extend many apologies along the way, but I was thriving.

Then suddenly, in what felt like the blink of an eye, they were all grown up, and my nest was empty, silent, and without meaning.

I slid headfirst into a funk of despair.

If I wasn't the mom driving kids to practices, shopping for prom dresses, and packing lunches . . . who was I?

Remember in the introduction when I said, "More on that later?" Here we go . . .

God spoke to me very directly through a pastor friend who said the reason I was spiraling was that I had been finding my identity and joy in things other than Him. I had put being a mom at the top of my priority list, above everything else, even God. And guess what? That's the actual definition of idolatry.

OUCH!

Seriously? Had I built a false god out of my role as a mom? As surely as if I had melted down all the gold in my neighborhood and sculpted a calf out of it. There was absolutely nothing wrong with me enjoying motherhood. Idolatry took root when it became the thing that I trusted to satisfy me instead of God.

Idolatry in any form will always be a joy blocker.

In the book of Jeremiah in the Old Testament, we find God's people in Israel having been rescued from slavery in Egypt, brought through the wilderness, and delivered to their own land, which had been promised to them. Other nations knew that Israel's God was a great God, and His temple had stood in Jerusalem for more than 300 years. Yet, the Israelites had turned from Him and worshiped other pagan gods.

Jeremiah 2:11 says, "Has any nation ever traded its gods for new ones, even though they are not gods at all? Yet my people have exchanged their glorious God for worthless idols!" Spoiler alert: The Israelites would soon find themselves in bondage after the Babylonians overtook their land.

How many times have we basked in the goodness of God, praised Him for His blessings and deliverance, and then turned around and poured our identity into something else?

An idol can take many forms, including material possessions, relationship status, social media attention, career success, and physical appearance. When we seek identity in *anything* other than Him, it becomes our god—it's our idol.

Matthew 22:37 tells us that when Jesus was asked what the most important commandment was, His reply was, "You must love the Lord your God with ALL your heart, ALL your soul, and ALL your mind" *(emphasis added)*.

If you're experiencing a joy deficit in your life, take a heart check. Is there anything in your heart, soul, or mind that is taking priority over God? Let's ensure the things we value don't become things we idolize.

Heavenly Father, I am so sorry for ever giving anything other than You top priority in my heart. Thank you for all of the people and things that You have blessed me with to love and enjoy, but please make it clear if I have placed too much value on them. I long to love You with all my heart, soul, and mind! Amen.

Questions for Reflection:
1. How would you describe the word "idolatry"?

NEXT STOP: Joy

2. Reread Matthew 22:37. It commands us to love God with all of our heart, mind, and soul. Which of these three can be the most difficult for you?

3. How would your life be different if you followed this command consistently?

Journal Prompt:
Write about the thing(s) you are most tempted to give idol status in your life. What are they? How can you keep them in their rightful place?

Day 16
We're Moving Here

"And it is impossible to please God without faith. Anyone who wants to come to Him must believe that God exists and that He rewards those who sincerely seek Him."
Hebrews 11:6 NLT

As my husband, Mike, and I stepped off the airplane, I looked at him and said, "We're moving here."

He immediately told me I was crazy. He hadn't even had the job interview, let alone an offer. But as soon as I took a deep breath of the salt air from the Gulf of Mexico, I felt God telling me that this would be our new home.

Mike had been running his own business for several years. I'd been working on and off, but was currently experiencing some struggles with autoimmune-related health issues. We both agreed that it was time for him to test the waters and see if a better option was available for us.

At the time, we lived in southern Ohio and decided we didn't want to move further south than Savannah, Georgia. Our daughters were four and six years old, and Mike and I's families lived nearby. We were very connected to them and wanted our girls to grow up making memories and basking in the love of their extended family.

So, when a company in the Tampa area offered to fly us down to Florida for an interview, I didn't take it too seriously. I was mostly just looking forward to getting a free trip to Clearwater Beach in the dead of winter.

Have you ever been to Ohio in February? It's the complete opposite of Florida.

This wasn't what I had in mind when I prayed for God to lead my husband to a good job that would use his talents and grow his career.

Have you ever done that? I prayed for God's will, yet I also gave Him guidelines for answering that prayer. Telling God what my answer should be is the exact opposite of faith.

Sure enough, they offered Mike the job, and just a few months later, we headed south to begin our new life. Saying goodbye to everyone and everything I knew was incredibly scary.

This is when I learned the difference between faith and belief. Believing something to be true is easy, but putting my trust and reliance in God's plan was an act of faith.

For example, I believed the airplane we boarded to travel to Tampa would take off, travel through the air, and land safely at our destination. However, I practiced faith when I boarded the plane, trusted the pilot, and embarked on the journey.

In 1 Samuel chapter 17, we read an incredible account of faith being put into action. Long before he became king, a shepherd boy named David was running an errand for his father when he learned that a giant had been insulting and taunting the Israelite army for over forty days.

The Philistine army had declared war against Israel. When David arrived on the scene, he found the two armies camped out, facing each other across a deep valley.

Goliath challenged them to send one man out to fight him for a winner-takes-all duel. But King Saul and his men were terrified of this larger-than-life champion. It's recorded that Goliath stood over nine feet tall. His helmet and armor alone weighed 125 pounds.

David was delivering food to his brothers when he heard about what was happening. He was deeply offended by Goliath's mocking of the Lord's people. He cared more about honoring God than the size of this enemy.

David volunteers to take the challenge, and fight the giant.

When King Saul questions his decision, David persists by recounting how God had always been faithful to him, even when he faced predators while tending his sheep. David recounted, "I have done this to both lions and bears, and I'll do it to this pagan Philistine, too, for he has defied the armies of the living God" (I Samuel 17:36)!

As we know, David takes his shepherd's staff, five rocks, and his slingshot out to face this enormous enemy.

David kills him with one shot after declaring, "The Lord will conquer you" (v 46).

David believed the God of Israel was above all and would protect him when he faced Goliath. He put his faith into action when he picked up the rocks and walked out to square off against a giant.

We've all had times when we're up against a circumstance or difficulty much bigger than us. Your "giant" might look different than mine, but the God we both put our faith in is the same.

Living a faith-in-action life is a direct line to joy. We can confidently face whatever uncertainty life throws us because, like David, we know we serve a victorious God.

NEXT STOP: Joy

Dear God, thank You for Your faithfulness. I pray that I'll be a woman who lives a faith-in-action life. I know there will be giants to fight, but I also know You will never leave me to face them alone. Thank you for all the times You have already gone to battle with me. I choose to walk by faith. Amen.

Questions for Reflection:
1. How is belief different from faith?

2. Read 1 Samuel 17. Why was David so confident he would win his battle with Goliath?

3. How can living a faith-in-action life lead to joy?

Journal Prompt:
Write about a "giant" you have faced or are currently facing. How has God been there with you through the battle?

_____

_____

_____

_____

_____

_____

_____

Day 17
Cheap Gold Paint

"Know that the Lord is God. It is He who made us, and we are His; we are His people the sheep of His pasture!"
Psalms 100:3, NIV

My grandpa was one of those guys who liked to tinker around in his workshop in his spare time. He had a small building in the backyard behind his house where he would spend hours working on his hobbies.

He was a communications specialist in World War II, so he especially enjoyed working on various radio-related devices. One of his favorite pastimes was restoring old radios, particularly those from the 1920s and 1930s, which featured a set of glass tubes that amplified the sound.

One afternoon, when my brother and I were around seven and eight years old, we were playing outside at our grandparents' house. We decided to enter Grandpa's shop to explore all of the interesting and mysterious things inside, and we came across a really old wooden radio that looked beat up and broken down.

We also happened upon a can of metallic gold spray paint.

I'm sure you know where this is going.

I don't remember which of us had the brilliant idea, but we decided the old radio would look amazing with a sparkly new coat of paint.

We really did have good intentions, but when we covered the antique with cheap gold paint, we completely ruined its value.

Isn't this basically what we do when we allow the things of this world to define who we are?

From the moment we're born, we're being evaluated. As girls, we learn early that the world finds us acceptable if we're pretty, intelligent, and likable.

Does our crush like us back? Did we make good grades? Are we popular?

When we let the world dictate our value, it can eventually affect how we perceive ourselves.

In John 4:5-30, we learn about a Samaritan woman on her way to draw water from the well who was dealing with that very issue. We never knew her name, but we believe she was an outcast.

Her race made her unacceptable to the Jews, her gender made her a second-class citizen in her society, and her past made her so ashamed that she traveled in the heat of the day in the desert to avoid interacting with others.

She finds a Jewish man already at the well on this particular day. He asks her for a drink of water, which is shocking in itself, but then he proceeds to tell her everything about herself. He shares with her that He is the Messiah and offers her living water—eternal life.

When she walked up to the well that afternoon, the woman believed she was useless. When she left, she ran to share the good news with everyone. She knew she had been cleansed from her past and made new.

NEXT STOP: *Joy*

A very good friend of mine recently shared with me that she had been struggling for quite some time with guilt and shame from her former life. During her prayer time one day, God spoke to her very pointedly, saying that she was no longer the woman at the well. She was forgiven; her past didn't define her.

That's the truth we all need.

At some point, we'll face the fact that we're broken, sinful individuals. But that doesn't have to be our identity.

When we accept God's gift of eternal life, we become women made new by the redemptive power of Jesus's blood. It changes everything!

Instead of using the "cheap gold paint" the world offers to make us think we're pleasing and acceptable, when we allow Jesus into our hearts, we live in the truth that we're forgiven of all of our sins, saved by grace, and unconditionally loved.

If we still find ourselves feeling broken and shameful on the inside, maybe it's because we are defining our value and worth in the things of this world instead of in Jesus.

Joy will follow when we embrace the truth of who Jesus says we are. "This means that anyone who belongs to Christ has become a new person. The old life is gone; a new life has begun!" (2 Corinthians 5:17, NLT).

Dear Jesus, Thank you for loving me enough to give your life so I can be made new. Help me to find my value in You alone. Today, I exchange my shame and guilt for forgiveness and healing. Please remind me of the truth when I start to listen to the world's lies. I am only who You say I am. Amen.

Questions for Reflection:
1. What are some ways the world tries to define you?

NEXT STOP: Joy

2. Read John 4:5-30. When in your life have you felt like the woman at the well - unclean and unworthy?

3. How does the promise in 2 Corinthians 5:17 impact how you see yourself?

Journal Prompt:
What is the contrast between who the world says you are and who Jesus says you are? Write out a declaration of truth based on 2 Corinthians 5:17.

Day 18
Tent City, NC

"Finally, all of you, be like-minded, be sympathetic, love one another, be compassionate and humble."
1 Peter 3:8 NIV

One of the many negative results of the COVID pandemic of 2020 was an increase in the homeless population of most major cities in the U.S. Job losses, skyrocketing housing costs, and social distancing in shelters contributed to a crisis that most cities weren't prepared for.

Charlotte, North Carolina, was no exception. By the winter of 2021, several homeless encampments had emerged, collectively becoming known as "tent city." The number of tents popping up along the north end of Charlotte expanded almost daily at an alarming rate.

It became increasingly impossible to ignore them when driving along the city's major interstates, so a group from our church decided we wanted to do something to help.

We organized a drive to collect sleeping bags to donate to the people living in the tents. Following an overwhelming response, we were thrilled to head downtown to distribute food and supplies.

NEXT STOP: Joy

I anticipated being moved by the experience of showing compassion to the less fortunate, but I wasn't prepared for the connection I would feel with them.

Their circumstances and their stories touched me incredibly.

I felt privileged to laugh with, pray for, and hug many of the homeless women. We joined hands, shed tears, and bonded over the details of their lives.

I knew our donations and generosity would benefit them, but when I left Tent City, I had a clearer view of Jesus than when I had entered.

One lady in particular left a lasting impression on me.

I had purchased a new winter jacket and water-resistant boots in preparation for spending the day outside in January, walking amongst the tents.

As we wandered around one segment of the encampment, I began talking to a woman who was expressing her gratitude for the donations and food being shared.

She told us her tent had flooded earlier in the week, and everything she owned was now covered in mud and mildew. She only had the clothes on her back to protect her from the winter temperatures.

Without hesitation, I removed my new coat and helped her put it on.

I don't share that to boast about my generosity. It really wasn't that great of a sacrifice. Even though I was cold for the rest of the day, I knew I would soon be headed home to a warm house.

I've never experienced that type of joy before—the kind that grows out of meeting the needs of someone who is suffering.

It was incredible! I felt like the Grinch when his heart grew three times its size.

It would have been easy just to see that she was cold and feel sorry for her.

How many times have we seen someone hurting or struggling, felt bad for them, but continued on our way, doing nothing about it?

We progress from empathy to compassion when we're moved into action.

Numerous displays of compassion mark Jesus' time on earth. A great example is found in Luke 7:11-15. Luke tells the story of a widow who had lost her only son.

Jesus and his disciples encountered her and the funeral procession as they approached the town gate of Nain.

Verse thirteen says Jesus "saw" her. That means He not only noticed her, but he cared about what she was experiencing. He had compassion for her sadness and took action. He walked over to the corpse of her son and said, "Young man, I say to you, get up!"

The son sat up and was returned to his mother.

I'm pretty certain most of us won't be called to travel from town to town and perform miracles, but there are opportunities all around us to show compassion.

Do we even know the needs of our family and friends? Do we have compassion for them and desire to help? Or are we more likely to be critical and judgmental?

I know I've been guilty at times of being too caught up in my own busyness to notice if someone is in need around me.

Let's commit to experiencing joy through showing compassion. We can start by asking God to reveal to us the needs of those people we encounter in our daily lives, and then actively move to help meet those deficiencies.

NEXT STOP: Joy

Lord, I'm sorry for all the times I've been too busy to notice the needs of those around me and for when I've been too self-involved to show compassion. Change my vision. Give me eyes that really "see" people. Help me to have a true desire to share Your love and joy by serving others. I want to be a woman of action, moving when you call me to move—showing mercy, kindness, and generosity in Your name. Amen.

Questions for Reflection:
1. What's the difference between empathy and compassion?

2. Read Luke 7:11-15. Why do you think Jesus approached the widow?

3. How do you receive joy when you show compassion to others?

Journal Prompt:
What are some current needs of friends and family members? Write down ways you can show compassion to them.

___

___

___

___

___

___

Day 19
Road Kill in July

"Consider it pure joy, my brothers and sisters, whenever you face trials of many kinds, because you know that the testing of your faith produces perseverance."
James 1:2-3, NLT

I will never forget the first time I saw the two solid pink lines pop up on a home pregnancy test. Within a matter of minutes, I ran through the entire gauntlet of emotions: shocked, ecstatic, joyful, and terrified all at once.

Everything was going along as expected until the beginning of my second trimester. I started experiencing high blood pressure, blurred vision, and swelling in my hands and feet.

By the time I was five months pregnant, I had to take a leave of absence from my job and was put on bed rest.

I was diagnosed with severe preeclampsia—a potentially dangerous condition.

Basically, I felt and looked like the Garfield balloon in the Macy's Thanksgiving Day parade. Some women glow and blossom during pregnancy—I blew up like road kill in July.

A couple of weeks before my due date, I was at my

doctor's appointment for a check-up. My symptoms had escalated, so I was sent to the hospital, and my labor was induced.

Fourteen hours later, our stubborn baby girl had yet to consider entering the world. By this time, my blood pressure had risen to stroke level.

The doctor concluded that I needed to have a cesarean birth. The baby was fine, but I was in danger.

About an hour later, the surgery was over, and Kylee Faith was showing off her healthy lungs and enjoying her first bath.

Everyone accompanied the nurse to coo over and cuddle baby Kylee. Everyone except for one person—my mom.

My condition remained critical as the hospital staff continued to work to get my blood pressure down to a safe number.

I don't really remember much about what happened after the surgery, but Mom told me later that she stayed by my side. She needed to make sure I was okay before she could revel in the excitement of her new granddaughter.

Even though I didn't know she was there, she never left me.

That's a beautiful reflection of our Heavenly Father.

Have you ever experienced an incredibly difficult time and wondered if God was with you?

The Bible promises us that He is and that He cares about what we're going through: "The Lord is close to the brokenhearted and saves those who are crushed in spirit" (Psalm 34:18, NLT).

Chapter three of Daniel shares an account of three men facing a life-threatening situation and how God intervened on their behalf.

Shadrach, Meshach, and Abednego were three Jewish

officials who had risen to high positions in Babylon. Other Babylonian officials were jealous of them and tattled to King Nebuchadnezzar that they weren't following his command.

They had refused to denounce God and bow down to worship the king's golden statue.

The king was furious and demanded that they be punished by being thrown into a fiery furnace seven times hotter than usual.

However, when King Nebachadnezzar looked into the fire, instead of seeing three men being tortured, he saw four men walking around in the furnace unharmed: Shadrach, Meshach, Abednego, and the Son of God.

The king called for them to come out of the furnace. They emerged from the fire unscathed, their hair unsinged and their clothing free of even the faintest hint of smoke.

The king then promoted the three Hebrew men and issued a decree that no one would be harmed for worshiping the God of Israel.

God not only saved them from certain death, but He brought good from their struggle.

That's why James 1:2-3 tells us, "Consider it pure joy, my brothers and sisters, whenever you face trials of many kinds, because you know that the testing of your faith produces perseverance."

It took me several decades to really understand what James was talking about in these verses. Are we really supposed to believe we should consider it a joy to face trials?

Absolutely, we are.

Not because the trials and suffering are enjoyable, but because "suffering produces perseverance; perseverance, character; and character, hope" (Romans 5:3-4).

Just like my daughter was the blessing that came out of

NEXT STOP: Joy

all of the difficulties I went through during my pregnancy, God has blessings waiting for you, too.

He will walk you through whatever "furnace" you are facing and help you grow in faith, character, and hope.

Heavenly Father, thank you for promising You are always with me, even when I feel alone. Thank you for using my suffering to grow perseverance, faith, character, and hope in me. I am sorry for the times I grumble and complain instead of reaching out and asking for strength and assurance from You. Amen.

Questions for Reflection:
1. What "furnace" are you walking through or have recently walked through?

2. Read Psalm 34:17-18. When have you experienced God's nearness while going through something difficult?

3. How can there be joy in trials (James 1:2-3)?

Journal Prompt:
Write about a time you experienced suffering or great difficulty. What blessings did God bring from it?

Day 20
A Juicy Secret

"We know that our old sinful selves were crucified with Christ so that sin might lose its power in our lives. We are no longer slaves to sin."
Romans 6:6, NLT

One afternoon, I was spending some quality time with an elderly lady whom I loved and admired. We were chit-chatting casually when she suddenly changed her demeanor, leaned in towards me, and whispered, "Nancy, I'm going to tell you something, but it has to stay between us."

I was immediately intrigued. I love getting the inside scoop on a juicy secret.

She shared with me that a stray animal had been causing her some problems. It had been finding a way through her fence and breaking into her storage shed.

The intruder had turned the interior of the building into its own personal restroom and was ruining everything inside.

No matter what she did, it found a way in.

She was a self-reliant, solve-my-own-problems gal. She had taken matters into her own hands and determined that this critter was not going to destroy her property.

She told me there had been a harmful liquid in a container in the building. She had decided to cut up a hot dog and put it in the liquid. (Please note: I do not condone this type of pest control; I'm only sharing her story.)

When she entered the building the next morning, the hot dogs and the trespasser were gone. She didn't know what ultimately happened, but it never returned.

I think it's a logical conclusion that the animal's desire for the hot dogs led to its demise.

How many times do we allow sin to control us similarly? We see something appealing and know it's not good for us, but we ingest it anyway.

Sin is inevitable. Romans 3:23 states, "For everyone has sinned; we all fall short of God's glorious standard."

However, because Jesus paid the ultimate sacrifice for our sins, we can be reconciled with God: "But if we confess our sins to Him, He is faithful and just to forgive us our sins and to cleanse us from all wickedness" (1 John 1:9).

The action phrase for us is "confess our sins to Him." Sin blocks us from joy when we leave it unaddressed and continue to repeat it.

While sin may seem enjoyable at first, it always has a destructive outcome, resulting in a ripple effect that harms our lives and potentially those of those around us. The guilt and shame that follow will result in us dodging God, leaving us void of the joy and peace He desires to provide.

To see this played out, we don't have to look further than

the first recorded sin in Genesis chapter three. Eve listened to the serpent's lies and saw that the tree was beautiful and its fruit looked delicious.

The Bible tells us, after eating the fruit God had commanded her not to touch, "immediately her eyes were open and she felt shame."

This was new to Eve. She had never experienced shame before, and it wasn't God's desire for her.

It's not His desire for us, either.

Let's take a spiritual inventory and ask God to reveal any unconfessed sin. Is there any sin we are actively participating in?

Do we download things on streaming platforms that we would never be seen watching in public?

Do we covet and judge others when scrolling through social media?

Do we sneak shopping bags into the house, hiding our spending from our spouse?

Do we gossip about and slander people who share different beliefs from ours? Or are we allowing our pride to keep us from apologizing to someone we know we have wronged?

Whatever sin we might be allowing in our lives, God is ready, willing, and able to offer us forgiveness. When we acknowledge and admit it to Him, the byproduct will be abundant joy.

Jesus, please forgive me for any sin I have been actively allowing to fester in my life. I confess my wrongdoing and rely on Your grace to free me. Silence the lies of guilt and shame from the enemy. Wash me clean and strengthen me as I go forward to sin no more. Amen.

NEXT STOP: Joy

Questions for Reflection:
1. Who does Romans 3:23 say has sinned?

2. What does 1 John 1:9 say we must do to be cleansed from sin?

3. Why is sin a joy blocker?

Journal Prompt:
Ask God if you are allowing anything in your life that is leading to sin. Then, spend a few minutes being still and listening. Write about what God reveals to you.

_____

_____

_____

_____

_____

_____

_____

_____

Day 21
Mommy, Is Santa Real?

"An honest witness tells the truth; a false witness tells lies."
Proverbs 12:17, NLT

When my youngest daughter was little, she hated any type of character in costume. She wanted nothing to do with Mickey and Minnie Mouse at Disney World, and seeing Santa Claus and the Easter Bunny in person usually resulted in her clutching on to me for dear life.

Because of this, I was entirely taken off guard when she approached me one December afternoon, a couple of months after her eighth birthday, and asked if I would take her to the mall to give Santa her Christmas list.

I was thrilled to share this magical experience with her, finally. We got ready and headed right over.

Before we got in line, my daughter, Macey, tugged on my hand, looked me in the eye, and asked, "Mommy, is Santa real?"

I wasn't prepared for that question. I took a breath, bent down, and replied, "Are you really sure you want me to answer that?"

She decided she didn't want to know just yet. So we continued on our mission.

When it was Macey's turn, she confidently approached Santa and hopped onto his lap. She didn't have much to say. Instead, she stared intensely at his face, trying to decide whether what she observed was authentic or fabricated.

Immediately after, she asked me again if Santa was real. I repeated my previous answer, but this time, she demanded that I come clean.

So I told her Santa Claus was a fictional character, and it was actually Daddy and I who had been putting the presents under the tree on Christmas morning.

Even though she said she wanted to know the truth, she wasn't prepared for it. She started crying and began firing off a long list of questions.

"Who had been eating the milk and cookies?"

"Was Frosty the Snowman real?"

"What about Rudolph?"

"Was the story of Baby Jesus true?"

She was questioning everything.

We returned to our car and were headed home when she burst into tears again and proclaimed, "Wait, does that mean the Easter Bunny and the Tooth Fairy aren't real either?"

She was devastated. Her world had been turned upside down.

Isn't that exactly how we respond when God reveals truth to us that we aren't comfortable hearing?

I especially don't like being told the truth about myself. I'm exceptionally gifted at spotting other people's faults more clearly than mine.

Over the last year, God has brought to my attention that my integrity wasn't where it needed to be. I wouldn't say I was dishonest, but follow-through was certainly not one of my strong suits.

I would mean something when I said it, but then I tended to get distracted, change my mind, or forget. God convicted me and revealed that these habits weren't pleasing to Him.

It stung a little.

I needed to issue some apologies, make amends in a few relationships, and submit to God's direction.

The story of Zacchaeus in Luke 19:1-10 highlights the value of honesty. You probably already know the song about the wee little man who climbed up in the sycamore tree.

Zacchaeus was a tax collector who became very rich, most likely by overcharging people and keeping the money for himself.

One day, Jesus was passing through his town, and Zacchaeus had a chance to meet him. In fact, Jesus went to his house and had dinner with him.

What happened next was nothing short of a miracle. Not only did he see the error of his ways, but Zacchaeus had a total change of heart. He gave away half of all his possessions and repaid people he had stolen from four times as much as he had taken.

He was transformed as a result of his encounter with Jesus. Living a dishonest life was no longer an option for him.

In a society where everyone is told they get to define their own "truth," honesty can lose its value. But the Bible teaches the contrary. Jesus says in John 8:32, "And you will know the truth, and the truth will set you free."

There is freedom in the truth, even when it's uncomfortable. If we desire a joy-filled life, we must live a life of honesty and integrity, not just when it's easy or convenient but also when it's not our own individual version of it.

Just because the idea of Santa Claus appealed to my daughter didn't make it true. If we're going to be women transformed by joy, we must live truthfully.

Dear Loving Father, I'm sorry for the times when I've let my desires and selfishness overshadow my integrity. Help me to be aware of when I'm bending or contorting the truth to meet my own agenda. Like Zacchaeus, I want to be transformed by my encounters with You. Lead me into a life overflowing with truth and honesty. Amen.

Questions for Reflection:
1. How would you define the word truth?

2. Read the story of Zacchaeus in Luke 19:1-10. Why was he different after spending time with Jesus?

3. How can dodging the truth be an obstacle to a joy-filled life?

Journal Prompt:
Where in your life do you struggle with honesty and integrity? What are some changes that God is leading you towards in those areas?

_____

_____

_____

_____

Day 22
Young, Dumb and In Love

*"Devote yourselves to prayer with an alert mind and
a thankful heart."*
Colossians 4:2, NLT

Every summer during college, I racked up an enormous long-distance phone bill. To work off my debt, I spent many hours washing cars and mowing the lawn.

I'm certain I still owe my dad a substantial amount of money.

You might remember that all calls had to be made through landlines before cell phones. If a phone call were made to someone outside of a defined local area, additional fees would be added to the monthly bill.

Because my college boyfriend lived several hours away, every time we would talk, it would be costly. Being young, dumb, and in love, I thought it was worth the expense.

Fast forward to the early 2000s, my husband and I moved our family across the country, and we now used cell phones to stay connected. Even though there was still a monthly charge, I could call my family and friends at any time without incurring any additional costs.

What a huge blessing that was! Any time I was lonely, excited, bored, or needed advice, I could call my mom. I was able to stay connected with loved ones without the dread of the phone bill showing up in the mailbox.

Currently, I'm incredibly grateful for the ability to FaceTime and text my daughters whenever I desire. I'm thrilled to be able to stay in constant connectivity with them as they attend school in different states.

As women, we are designed to be connected.

How many times a day do we connect to something? Wi-Fi, Bluetooth, a phone charger, a cell tower — it's constant. We live in a world that is more connected now than ever before in history.

The most important connection we have, however, is the one with God. Prayer is a way for us to stay in constant connection with Him. Jesus modeled this during His time on earth, and in 1 Thessalonians 5:17, Paul instructs us to "Never stop praying."

Jesus teaches His disciples about the importance of being persistent in prayer in Luke 18:1-8.

The parable tells us about a determined widow and an unjust judge who presides over her town. In a Jewish community, the judge was expected to be fair and recognize that judgment ultimately belongs to God.

The needy widow of the story repeatedly came before the judge to plead her case. According to the law, widows were supposed to be cared for and given special protection. This judge, however, was ignoring her. He didn't care about her or her circumstances. Time after time, he continued to dismiss her case.

The widow refused to give up. She continued to present her case before the judge repeatedly.

It would appear she annoys him to the point of wearing him down. Eventually, the judge says to himself, "I don't fear God or care about people, but this woman is driving me crazy. I'm going to see that she gets justice because she is wearing me out with her constant requests" (v. 4-5).

The woman finally got the justice she was seeking.

Jesus then elaborates on his point. If an uncaring, ungodly, unfit judge eventually gives justice in the end, how much more will your loving Heavenly Father give to His devoted children?

Faithful, persistent, never-ceasing prayer should be a watermark in every Christian woman's life. Like the widow, we are needy and dependent on God to bring order and meaning to our lives.

Jesus knew we would go through discouraging and confusing times. He knew we would face difficult circumstances and would be tempted to give up. He shared this story to encourage us to stay in a nonstop, purposeful, and mindful state of prayer.

Joy can be found in the divine connectivity of prayer. We have the assurance that we are never alone, always being heard and continually fastened in communication with the God of the universe.

Heavenly Father, thank you for creating me to be connected. Thank you for the gift of prayer. Help me to abide in communication with You. In a world where so many things are vying for my attention, I want to hear You above all else. Amen.

Questions for Reflection:

1. In what ways do you stay connected to people in your life?

NEXT STOP: Joy

2. Read the parable in Luke 18:1-8. What is Jesus teaching us about prayer?

3. How can you stay more connected to God?

Journal Prompt:
Write about a time in your life when being connected to someone was a blessing to you. How does knowing you have a constant connection to God produce joy in your life?

Day 23
Sunny Bunny

"If you love Me, obey My commandments."
John 14:15 NLT

If I had to describe myself, being a "dog person" would be pretty high up on the list. I've never been without at least one beloved canine.

I've loved them all, but some of them have left bigger imprints on my heart than others. One exceptionally special pup was a blonde labradoodle that I gave to my husband for our fifth wedding anniversary. Her name was Sunny Miami, but we lovingly referred to her as Sunny Bunny.

She had the kindest heart and most gentle disposition of any dog I've ever owned. She was loyal and fun-loving. Her intelligence and desire to please her people were unmatched.

When my visually challenged nephew came to visit us, she instinctively and proudly guided him around the house. We concluded it was no longer productive to put her in a crate when we left the house, because she would always figure out how to escape. Upon leaving, we would double-check that both latches were secure, but when we returned, we would find her lounging on the couch like a fluffy, curly-topped Houdini.

She followed many verbal commands and could perform multiple tricks. My favorite was putting a dog treat on top of her nose, and when I said, "OK," she would toss the treat up into the air and catch it.

She reveled in the accolades and "good girls." She was always obedient and followed every direction given to her without hesitation.

What if we possessed that same type of commitment to following God's commands? What if we trusted He knew best, and without pause, walked in obedience with Him?

Luke 1:26-38 highlights the obedience of a young Jewish girl named Mary.

Mary was in the middle of planning her wedding to a carpenter named Joseph when she was visited by the angel, Gabriel. He tells her, "You will conceive and give birth to a son, and you will name Him Jesus" (Luke 1:31).

It's easy for us to get so excited by the birth of Jesus in the Christmas story that we overlook the difficult position Mary was in.

She had to tell her fiancé she was pregnant even though they had never been intimate. She had to face the possibility of gossip, poverty, and even death. I imagine she would have been easily overwhelmed by stress and emotion.

However, Mary didn't let fear overcome her. Instead, negative thoughts seem to be the furthest from her mind when she responds in verses 46-49, "Oh, how my soul praises the Lord. How my spirit rejoices in God my Savior! For He took notice of His lowly servant girl, and from now on all generations will call me blessed. For the Mighty One is holy, and He has done great things for me."

My first response to doing something difficult has never been to rejoice. Mary didn't counter by trying to give God all the reasons why she wasn't qualified. She didn't roll her eyes and drag her feet. She didn't pout and whine, asking God, "Why?"

Mary REJOICED!

She refers to herself as God's servant. She was able to obey so immediately and wholeheartedly because she knew her position. She knew who God was and desired to live a life of service to Him.

If it's really that simple, why is obedience such a struggle? A common obstacle is pride. We don't always like being told what to do and how to do it.

Sometimes we're hesitant because it's inconvenient. (I don't think it gets any more problematic than Mary's circumstances.)

Disobedience can also be rooted in stubbornness and selfish desire. Do we really want God's best for us? Or like Sunny, do we keep trying to sneak out of whatever restrictions we've been given? Disobedience will always be a detour to joy.

However, the fruit of obedience is that we'll remain in union with God, and the unity we have with Him will undoubtedly lead to a joy-filled life.

Heavenly Father, thank you so much for the beautiful example of obedience in Mary's response to being called to be the mother of Jesus. I desire to live a life with the same willing and rejoicing heart. Please remove any stubbornness, pride, or selfishness that may be a stumbling block to obeying You. I want to please you, Lord, in every area of my life. Amen.

Questions for Reflection:
1. How would you describe obedience?

NEXT STOP: Joy

2. Read Luke 1:26-38. How did Mary respond to what the angel told her?

3. How might there be joy in obedience to God?

Journal Prompt:
Write about a time when you were faced with the challenge of obedience. What lessons did you learn?

_____

_____

_____

_____

_____

_____

_____

_____

_____

_____

Day 24
Big Picture God

"I pray that God, the source of hope, will fill you completely with joy and peace because you trust Him. Then you will overflow with confident hope through the power of the Holy Spirit."
Romans 15:13, NLT

When my niece and youngest nephew were just beginning elementary school, they were diagnosed with Juvenile Batten Disease. It's a rare, inherited neurodegenerative disorder that usually develops between the ages of five and ten.

Children with Juvenile Batten Disease suffer from blindness, seizures, delayed developmental milestones, and a loss of language and motor skills.

There is currently no treatment or cure. It's always fatal, with most children not living beyond their teens or early twenties.

The summer after my niece passed away, I accompanied my sister-in-law to Chicago to attend the BDSRA (Batten Disease Support & Research) conference. It was an event that the foundation organized annually to foster a strong community of support for families affected by this disease.

As we entered the lobby of the accommodating hotel, I

was taken aback by the immense sense of belonging. This was a group of people who were often isolated and consumed by the daily struggles their children faced. It was strangely both comforting and heartbreaking to observe them coming together, bonded by their tragic diagnoses.

There were so many things I will never forget about that weekend, but one of the most unexpected takeaways was the overwhelming power of hope.

On the first morning, there was an opportunity to meet with many of the doctors and researchers who were committed to understanding the disease. They shared new discoveries and developments from their research, and although they didn't have it all figured out, they had made some small steps in understanding it and unraveling the mystery.

They provided something that every single person in that room needed. Although there was still no cure, progress was being made. They were closer.

It was something. It was hope.

Have you ever found yourself in a place that seemed utterly hopeless, but then a small glimmer of hope was spotted? It doesn't take much. Hope is powerful. Even the slightest whisper of it can completely alter our perspective.

Hope implies confidence in the possibility of a certain thing happening. There's a desire and an expectation.

The story of Joseph, found in Genesis chapters 37-50, is an unexpected testament to hope amidst difficulty and disappointment.

Joseph is the favorite of twelve sons. His brothers hate him. They beat him up, toss him into a hole, then sell him into slavery.

It gets a lot worse for him before it gets better.

NEXT STOP: Joy

Joseph is taken to Egypt, where he becomes a steward to one of Pharaoh's officials. The official's wife makes false accusations against him, and he winds up in prison.

Because Joseph is able to interpret one of Pharaoh's dreams, he is made the governor of Egypt. This put him in a position to ration the country's food supply to prepare for a time of famine.

During the eventual famine, his brothers unknowingly come to him asking for food. After twenty-two years of ups and downs, Joseph is able to save his family from starvation.

When Joseph finally reveals his identity to his brothers, he tells them not to be too hard on themselves. He said, "God has sent me ahead of you to keep you and your families alive and preserve many survivors" (Genesis 45:7).

Joseph was able to maintain hope during all his struggles because he knew that, no matter how it seemed at the time, God was still in control.

He was able to hold on to hope because he knew that God was greater than his disappointments and difficulties. Joseph knew that he served a "Big Picture God"—a God who was ultimately working all things together for good even when it appeared that He wasn't.

Romans 8:28 says, "And we know that God causes everything to work together for the good of those who love God and are called according to His plan."

What area of your life needs an injection of hope? Regardless of how things appear, you can find joy in knowing that God is at work and in control.

Dear God, thank you for the truth that no matter how things seem in my life, You alone are in control. I'm sorry for the times I choose to focus on fear and frustration instead of hope. Help me to remember that You are always at work in my circumstances. I find joy today in the knowledge that all things work together through You.

Questions for Reflection:

1. What does the word "hope" mean to you?

2. Read Genesis 45:1-15. After everything that he went through, why was Joseph able to be happy when he reunited with his brothers?

3. How can having hope produce joy?

Journal Prompt:

When has hope been an important factor in your life? Write about a time when you needed it most.

_____

_____

_____

_____

_____

_____

Day 25
The MVP

"Don't put it off; do it now! Don't rest until you do."
Proverbs 6:4, NLT

At 8:30 p.m. on most Tuesday evenings in the mid-to-late seventies, I could be found sitting in front of our family's television watching *Welcome Back Kotter*. It was a half-hour sitcom set in an ethnically diverse high school in Brooklyn, New York.

The main character, Mr. Kotter, was a teacher who returned to his alma mater in an attempt to educate a group of challenged high school students—lovingly known as the "sweathogs."

It was a lighthearted show that typically followed the high jinks of the dumb-but-lovable students in Mr. Kotter's class. The cast of students was entertaining and included a wisecracking ladies' man named Vinnie Barbarino, played by a young John Travolta.

The popular show led to many classic catchphrases. (If you're a Gen X'er, you might have insulted someone by declaring, "Up your nose with a rubber hose!").

One of my favorites occurred whenever Vinnie was confronted with a situation that he didn't want to address. He would take on a confused persona and respond with a simple, wide-eyed, "What?" Regardless of what the answer was, he always followed up with an equally clueless, "Where?"

When was the last time you were faced with something and instead of dealing with it head-on, you chose to give the classic Vinnie Barbarino response?

I'm definitely quick to side-step something that makes me uncomfortable.

Logically, I know that by avoiding and putting things off, I'm increasing stress in my life—but emotionally, I prefer to look the other way and pretend that it's not there.

Can you relate? What on your to-do list are you currently dodging?

Generally speaking, I don't think this creates a moral dilemma, but over time, the consequence will be that joy will begin to seep out of our lives.

Living an avoidance lifestyle will inevitably become a joy blocker.

The book of Jonah, found in the Old Testament, gives an incredible account of an Israelite man who is the MVP of avoidance.

In chapter one, God tells Jonah to visit the great city of Nineveh and preach to them because they were very wicked. Jonah wanted nothing to do with this assignment.

He attempts to avoid God's calling by jumping on a boat that was headed in the opposite direction. It says, "but the Lord hurled a powerful wind over the sea, causing a violent storm that threatened to break the ship apart" (Jonah 1:4, NLT).

The sailors decided it was Jonah's running from God that caused the storm, so they threw him overboard. As soon as they plopped Jonah into the water, the storm stopped.

God then sent a whale-like fish to swallow Jonah and save him from drowning. Jonah spent three days in the belly of the fish. During that time, he prayed to God and begged for help. He repented for his actions and finally praised God.

After three days, God made the fish regurgitate Jonah onto the shore. God again commands him to go to Nineveh. This time, Jonah obeyed.

Jonah delivered God's message, "Forty days from now, Nineveh will be destroyed!" The people believed and repented, turning from their evil ways. God showed mercy on them, and the city was saved from destruction.

Imagine all that Jonah would have avoided if he had just obeyed the first time God approached him.

How much time and energy do we waste because we avoid doing what we know needs to be done? How much stress and anxiety are we adding to our lives because we don't want to face something that's difficult?

If we're eliminating everything that is a barrier to living a joy-filled life, then we must eliminate "avoidance."

Avoidance is more than just a coping mechanism—it's a harmful behavior the enemy can use to cultivate fear, anxiety, and unhealthy habits in our lives.

Much like Jonah's voyage was an attempt to go in the opposite direction of Nineveh, avoidance will have us drifting in the reverse direction of joy.

Dear Heavenly Father, thank You for being a patient and loving God. I know that so many times I've hesitated to respond to Your direction. Help me to face whatever needs to be

NEXT STOP: Joy

done with confidence and assuredness because I know You are with me. Reveal to me anything in my life that is currently an avoidance response. Amen.

Questions for Reflection:
1. What do you think is the opposite of avoidance?

2. Read Jonah 1:1-3. What was Jonah's response when God gave him a specific assignment?

3. Why do we sometimes choose avoidance instead of obedience?

Journal Prompt:
What part of Jonah's story do you relate to the most? Write about a time when avoidance caused a problem to compound a situation in your life. How could you react in faith instead?

Day 26
Pepper and Darkness

"The light shines in the darkness, and the darkness can never extinguish it."
John 1:5, NLT

I was blessed to drive my daughters to school almost every day from kindergarten through their senior years. Although I'm the furthest thing from a morning person, I always looked forward to those twenty minutes we had alone on our commute.

We definitely had many "Hurry up, we're going to be late!" and "Where's your backpack?" moments—but they were greatly overshadowed by the joy of starting our days together.

We always prayed and listened to worship music to set our hearts and minds right for whatever the day had in store for us.

Without fail, as the girls opened their doors to exit the car, I would call out a reminder, "Be the salt and the light!" (A reference to Matthew 5:13-15).

One morning, one of my daughters looked back over her shoulder and responded sarcastically, "Today I'm feeling more like pepper and darkness."

This became a recurring joke for many years to come. It was funny because it was true.

Some days we aren't feeling like the salt and the light. Have you ever had a "pepper and darkness" kind of day? I certainly have!

God reminds us repeatedly in the Scriptures just how important "light" is.

The very first thing God did after creating the heavens and the earth was to separate darkness from light. Genesis 1:3 says, "Then God said, 'Let there be light,' and there was light."

Light serves many purposes. It illuminates our way, shines truth amid lies, eliminates fear, and provides a place for growth and encouragement.

In John 8:12, Jesus is letting us know He is the exclusive source of spiritual light, saying, "I am the light of the world. If you follow me, you won't have to walk in darkness, because you will have the light that leads to life."

That's the ultimate power source.

But it's not enough for us to just walk in the light. We are called to share it with others.

Matthew 5:14-15 tells us that Jesus said, "You are the light of the world, like a city on a hilltop that cannot be hidden. No one lights a lamp and then puts it under a basket. Instead, a lamp is placed on a stand, where it gives light to everyone in the house."

Consider the placement of lamps in your home. What's their purpose? How ridiculous would it be to place a lamp under your bed? Or cover one with a box?

That's what we're doing if we are Christians but aren't sharing our light outwardly. We're not supposed to keep it for ourselves. Jesus tells us to "place it on a stand" so everyone can see.

How do we do that practically? It's reflected primarily in the way we love others.

Do we care more about our day than the impact we're having on someone else?

Do we overschedule our lives so much that there's no room to pour into someone living in darkness?

Have we even considered who needs to see God's light? Have we made them a priority?

It's like discovering the most amazing restaurant, then taking all your friends there to share the experience with you.

This is multi-faceted joy. We experience joy by basking in God's light, truth, and goodness, and joy is also the by-product of sharing God's light with others.

Dear God, thank you for sending Your son, Jesus, to be the Light of the World. I'm forgiven for my shortcomings because of His sacrifice on my behalf. Show me where I need to shine this Good News today. Make me aware of where You're calling me to shine for You. Amen.

Questions for Reflection:
1. In John 8:12, why is Jesus described as "the Light of the World"?

NEXT STOP: Joy

2. Who is Jesus talking to in Matthew 5:14-15?

3. How are you sharing God's light in your life?

Journal Prompt:
Where do you need to shine brighter today? Who needs to see Jesus shining in you? How will you go about doing that?

Day 27
I've Never Owned a Boat

"Put on your new nature, created to be like God - truly righteous and holy"
Ephesians 4:24 NLT

I may never have been mistaken for a fashionista, but I've always loved to be in the know of what's new and trendy. I used to wait in anticipation every month for the latest issues of *Glamour* and *Seventeen* magazines.

As a teenager in the 1980s, I unapologetically embraced many questionable fashion trends.

I argued with my mom over the necessity of acquiring designer jeans. They had to have a specific label and had to be purchased from an exclusive store.

I would spend my entire back-to-school shopping budget on shirts with the little alligator logo, and even though I had never owned a boat, "boat shoes" were a must.

My watch could only be a Swatch. My jean jacket had to be oversized, and by my senior year of high school, MTV became my guide to everything cool.

I even double-pierced a single earlobe in an attempt to emulate the edginess of the young pop-star sensation, Janet Jackson.

All of this was really just a desperate attempt to fit in—to be included. I was terrified of the agonizing feeling of loneliness, which I assumed accompanied being different.

I attended three high schools and was often the new girl on the first day of fall classes. This created a deep sense of not belonging anywhere.

So I would continually reinvent myself with the goal of blending in.

When was the last time you felt set apart? Not part of the group?

It wasn't until I was much older (and hopefully wiser) that I realized "fitting in" wasn't really part of God's design for us. As women of God, we *should* be standing apart from the world. God showed me how being different and being lonely weren't the same thing. In fact, God uses our uniqueness to bring Him glory.

The story of Esther, found in the book of the same name in the Old Testament, tells a remarkable tale of how God uses a young Jewish girl to save His chosen people.

Esther is described as beautiful and obedient.

While keeping her Jewish identity a secret, the king, Ahasuerus, falls in love with her and makes her his queen.

After she becomes queen, her cousin, Mordecai, becomes involved in a power struggle with the king's right-hand man, Haman, who made it his personal goal to destroy all of the Jews.

Esther eventually reveals the plot to the king. His love for his queen motivates him to save her people.

NEXT STOP: *Joy*

All of this resulted because Esther's God-given uniqueness made her stand apart from the rest of the harem.

Esther was in the right place at the right time because she didn't "fit in."

For many years, I had it backwards. The more I blended in with the world around me, the happier I would be.

But God created us to be one-of-a-kind masterpieces, not clones of popular culture.

Joy is found in embracing the truth found in Isaiah 64:8, "And yet, O Lord, You are our Father. We are the clay, and You are the potter. We all are formed by Your hand."

The Master Creator intentionally chose every part of us. Join me today in embracing the uniqueness of who God created you to be.

Dear God, thank you for reminding me that it's not Your will for me to fit into this world. Help me to remember that I am the clay and You're the potter. Mold and shape me into Your one-of-a-kind design. I desire to fulfill Your good and perfect will for my life. Continue to show me the beauty in the uniqueness of myself and others. Thank you for being such a creative and loving Father. Amen.

Questions for Reflection:

1. Read Isaiah 64:8 again. What do you think it means when it says we are the clay and God is the potter?

2. How does this change how you see yourself? And others?

NEXT STOP: Joy

3. How can not fitting in lead to increased joy in your life?

Journal Prompt:
Write about a time in your life when you struggled with feeling like you didn't fit in. How has your perspective changed after reading Isaiah 64:8?

Day 28
Playing Princess

"And now, just as you accepted Christ Jesus as your Lord, you must continue to follow Him."
Colossians 2:6 NLT

About ten miles outside of Lexington, Kentucky, is a most unusual landmark. Nestled amongst acres of horse farms, bourbon distilleries, and Wildcat basketball fans is a four-star luxury hotel and spa located inside a real-life castle.

The Kentucky Castle began construction in 1968 as a labor of love when a young couple was mesmerized by the old European structures they had seen on their honeymoon. Unfortunately, they never saw their vision come to life because they divorced before it was completed.

However, in 2008, a group of investors purchased the property and transformed it into the magnificent destination it is today.

The castle sits on fifty-three lush acres of land and is adjacent to a working farm that supplies food for its restaurant located on the ground floor.

I thought it would be fun to take my oldest daughter there to celebrate the completion of her master's degree. What

NEXT STOP: Joy

could be better than playing princess for a few days?

We booked a stay at a little cabin located on the farm overlooking the castle. It was like a storybook come to life. There were adorable baby farm animals, soft, warm breezes, wild lavender, and (did I mention) a spa.

On the first morning of our stay, I sat on our front porch, eating my breakfast and taking it all in. As I gazed at the castle in the distance, I felt God whispering, "This is how you spent many years with Me—you wanted to be near Me but separate from Me."

My eyes welled up with tears as I realized how true that was.

I'd given my life to the Lord when I was a young teenager, but I spent the next several decades attempting to serve Him on my terms. I had a glimpse of His goodness, but I kept myself at a distance, stubbornly trying to maintain a mirage of control.

I loved God, but I wasn't abiding in Him.

Have you ever hesitated to commit fully to God? You had accepted His grace but then chose to keep Him at arm's length?

In John chapter fifteen, Jesus gives us a beautiful parable about the importance of abiding in the Lord: "Remain in Me, and I in you. For a branch cannot produce fruit if it is severed from the vine, and you cannot be fruitful unless you remain in me, and I in them, will produce much fruit. For apart from me you can do nothing" (John 15:4-5).

We are the branches, and Jesus is the vine.

What happens when a branch is cut from the vine? It may be able to live for a short period, but eventually it will wither from a lack of nourishment.

Jesus tells us that we must abide in and remain connected to Him to continue growing and producing healthy fruit.

Abiding is not what saves us, but it will sustain us.

Jesus says that if we want to continue to grow and flourish, we have to remain in Him.

That sounds awesome, but how do we actually do that?

One of the easiest habits to adopt is spending time in prayer every day, consistently and authentically.

We also abide in the Lord by reading and studying the Bible. It's our instruction manual and love letter. The Bible provides us with direction, insight into the nature of God, and a deeper understanding of our purpose.

Another great way to stay connected to the Vine is by serving His people. Get involved in a ministry. It will require you to lean on God more and grow in a deeper relationship with Him.

I think it's safe to say that if given the option, we would all choose to take up residence in the luxury castle instead of the gruff, tiny cabin overlooking its beauty. But that's exactly what we're doing if we live a life that's not connected consistently to our Lord and Savior.

Abiding in the Lord will produce the ripe, bountiful fruit of joy.

What is your current address? Are you a bystander, looking at what God has in store for you from afar? Or are you electing to thrive as a true daughter of the King?

Heavenly Father, I want to learn to abide in You. I desire to live a life connected to the Vine. I want all You have for me. Please lead me into daily, authentic habits that will allow me to grow in a deeper relationship with You. Amen.

NEXT STOP: Joy

Questions for Reflection:

1. Read John 15:1-5. Although Jesus is directly speaking to His disciples, how does this passage apply to us as believers?

2. What does it mean to "abide" in Christ? What are the three practical ways to do that?

3. How does abiding produce joy in our lives?

Journal Prompt:

What things in your life are holding you back from staying connected to the Vine? Write out a plan of action on how you will intentionally abide in Him daily.

_____

_____

_____

_____

_____

_____

_____

Day 29
A Coveted Carnival Prize

"Trust in the Lord with all your heart; do not depend on your own understanding"
Proverbs 3:5, NLT

One of the most unique pets I've ever owned was a goldfish named Jeffrey. Jeffrey wasn't just any ordinary fish–he was a coveted carnival prize that had been won by my youngest daughter successfully tossing a ping pong ball into his bowl.

What made Jeffrey unique wasn't how we had obtained him or any of his outstanding physical features—he was special because he continued, over and over again, to try to escape his fishbowl.

I'm not a fish expert, but I'm pretty sure most of them aspire to exist in the very water that gives them life.

But not Jeffrey.

He would swim as fast as he could to gain momentum and repeatedly crash into the side of his bowl as if to attempt to break out of the glass prison.

And I still don't know exactly how he did it, but somehow Jeffrey would catapult himself into the air, hoping to

NEXT STOP: Joy

jump out of his home. There would be small puddles of water all around it from the failed attempts.

As I watched his bizarre behavior, it occurred to me that this is what we must look like to God when we disregard the direction He has given us.

Have you ever found yourself in a rough spot because you ignored what God said and took matters into your own hands?

Sarah, the wife of Abraham, certainly did. Her story, found in Genesis, is quite the adventure—complete with many plot twists and turns.

Sarah faithfully followed her husband as he went about the Lord's calling on his life to lead His people into the Promised Land.

We know Sarah was beautiful and wealthy. She had a blessed life, but she was desperate for children. She had been barren for many years and was struggling to wait on the promise which God revealed to her husband in Genesis 17:16, "And I will bless her richly, and she will become the mother of many nations. Kings of nations will be among her descendants."

Sarah was sixty-five years old when Abraham was first promised a son. She had to wait twenty-five long years before that promise was fulfilled.

Sarah got impatient and decided to take matters into her own hands. Rather than waiting for God's timing, Sarah suggests that Abraham should sleep with her servant girl, Hagar.

Hagar became pregnant, and Sarah was overcome with jealousy, leaving her more miserable than she was before.

Several years later, three men, who were actually angels, approached Abraham.

After sharing a meal with him, one of the angels makes a

proclamation, "I will return to you about this time next year, and your wife, Sarah, will have a son!" (Genesis 18:10).

Sarah was listening at the door and laughed (probably in disbelief) at this announcement. She would have been eighty-nine years old. I'm sure she had given up hoping for God to fulfill His promise.

As always, God was faithful, and a year later, their son, Isaac, was born.

Sarah could have avoided so much pain and unpleasantness if she had just trusted in the Lord and submitted to His plan.

Like Sara, most of us have attempted to help God out by trying to control a situation instead of waiting for His timing.

What is God asking you to trust Him with today? Are you being faithful in the waiting, or like Jeffrey, are you repeatedly trying to find a way out of it?

We can find joy in the truth that God is in control and His timing is always perfect.

Dear Heavenly Father, thank you for the truth that You are always in control. I'm sorry for the times when I attempt to take the reins instead of submitting to you. I believe You are good and perfect. I know You don't need me to fulfill Your will, but I am grateful You allow me to be a part of Your plan. Amen.

Questions for Reflection:
1. Read Genesis 18:1-14. Why do you think Sarah responded the way she did?

NEXT STOP: Joy

2. Why can waiting for God's timing be difficult?

3. How can you find joy in the waiting?

Journal Prompt:
Write about a time when you took matters into your own hands instead of waiting on God. What lessons did you learn as a result? How would you approach things differently now that you know what you know?

Day 30
Furniture for Christmas?

"For I know the plans I have for you," says the Lord. "They are plans for good and not for disaster, to give you a future and a hope."
Jeremiah 29:11, NLT

When I was eleven years old, I decided to play detective and attempted to find my Christmas presents before the big reveal on the morning of December twenty-fifth.

My brother and I usually returned home from school several hours before our parents did, so I had the perfect opportunity to snoop.

I peered into all of the obvious places, and eventually I found what I was looking for.

Hidden away in my parents' bedroom closet were two enormous boxes that had already been completely covered in Christmas wrapping paper.

I was so excited!

I had no idea what was inside the large packages, but I concluded that it had to be something amazing.

I immediately shared my discovery with my friends and asked for their input on what the gift could possibly be. They came up with some great possibilities, but one of them told me not to get my hopes up. It was probably just a chest of drawers for my bedroom.

Seriously?

Unfortunately, it made sense. That was exactly the size of the box.

I was so disappointed. I instantly went from being excited to open my big gift to dreading it.

How could my parents do that? Who would give a kid furniture for Christmas?

Eventually there was no avoiding it.

It was time to unwrap the present. I begrudgingly tore the paper off the package to expose what was inside.

Imagine my overwhelming surprise when I discovered that my mom and dad had actually bought me a beautiful, state-of-the-art stereo system—complete with dual cassette players.

It was awesome!

Better than anything I'd imagined.

Despite my exhilaration, I heard a nagging voice in the back of my head rebuking me for my previous bratty behavior.

Why couldn't I just be grateful regardless of what I was being given? Why didn't I have confidence that my parents knew what would be good for me?

That's exactly what we're doing when we're scared to trust God's plans for us. Have you ever been afraid that what God has for you will be different from what you want?

The story of the rich man in Matthew 19:16-22 is a biblical

account of a young man who lets his fear get the best of him.

We're told the man approached Jesus and asked Him what he needed to do to have eternal life.

Matthew recounts that the man had been faithful in keeping all of God's commandments and believed Jesus knew the way to heaven.

Jesus replied to his question, "If you want to be perfect, go and sell all your possessions and give the money to the poor, and you will have treasure in heaven. Then come, follow me" (Matthew 19:21).

When the young man heard this, the bible says he went away sad because he was very wealthy and didn't want to give all of his stuff away.

Usually, when this story is referenced, it's to emphasize how the love of money can lead to our downfall.

That's definitely an important lesson, but I think fear is really at the root of the man's decision. He was afraid to trust Jesus with the unknown. He liked his life and all of his belongings. It was safe and familiar.

Fear triumphs over faith when we refuse to take the next step if we can't see where it's leading. We don't *really* trust God if we're only obedient when we're confident of the outcome.

Fear is one of the enemy's most effective weapons to block the joy in our lives. This is mainly because it separates us from God—the more we feed into it, the less we trust Him.

What unknown have you been hesitant to surrender to God? Are you afraid to give Him control of your career? Your relationships? Your children?

Let's not allow fear to rob us of the joy God has for us. Let's collectively unwrap the gift of God's plans for us with faith-filled enthusiasm, trusting that it will glorify Him and fulfill His perfect and loving will for our lives.

Dear Heavenly Father, I want to trust You completely. Please show me where I'm allowing fear to hold me back from following Your plans for me. I desire to surrender myself entirely to you. I don't want fear to rob me of the joy that can be found only in You. Thank you for the promise that Your plans for me are good, to give me hope and a future. Amen.

Questions for Reflection:
1. Read Matthew 19:16-22. What is the young man seeking?

2. With what areas of your life are most difficult to trust God?

3. How does fear rob you of joy?

Journal Prompt:
What has been something you've struggled to trust God's plan with? Write a letter to Him confessing that fear. Tell Him what you're afraid of and make a promise to trust Him now.

___

___

___

___

___

NEXT STOP: Joy

NEXT STOP: Joy

Continuing the Journey

YOU DID IT! You've completed the first leg of your joy journey! I trust God has renewed, redeemed, and rejoiced with you along the way.

You've been convicted and forgiven.

You've received healing and direction.

I hope you've been able to laugh and cry with me as I've shared all that God revealed to me as I traveled this incredible road with Him.

When I first started this book, I assumed He had taught me all I needed to know about living a joy-filled life. I expected to type it all out, send it to my publisher, and celebrate the completion of my work.

It's now been a little over two years since I began my endeavor.

God has revealed to me very loudly that this is a lifelong quest. Joy isn't something that can be acquired and dusted off whenever we need a quick fix of it. It's a daily pruning and surrendering. It's a day-by-day (sometimes minute-by-minute) refining less of me, more of Him.

I invite you to join me in continuing to seek God's perfect and life-giving joy. Here are four practical ways to ensure you reach the holy destination of a joy-saturated life.

NEXT STOP: *Joy*

1. ***What's the real goal:*** *"Trust in the Lord with all your; heart; do not depend on your own understanding. Seek His will in all you do, and He will show you which path to take"* (Proverbs 3:5-6).

    First, we need to ensure that we're letting God reveal His definition of joy. He's the Ultimate Creator; therefore, He's the one who constructs joy. Let's ensure we are authentically seeking His joy, not just chasing feelings and desires.

2. ***Daily workouts:*** *"I will praise You as long as I live, lifting up my hands to You in prayer. You satisfy me more than the richest feast. I will praise You with songs of joy"* (Psalms 63:4-5).

    Spending time in God's presence daily is the most effective way to stay connected to Him. The Bible assures us He is everywhere at all times. But if we don't make a conscious effort to be alone with Him, our joy-basins will run dry. The Holy Spirit is ready and willing to be a constant source of renewal.

3. ***Get to it:*** *"In His kindness God called you to share in His eternal glory by means of Christ Jesus. So after you have suffered a little while, He will restore, support, and strengthen you, and He will place you on a firm foundation"* (1 Peter 5:10-11).

    What have you side-stepped or ignored? Is there any lingering or unaddressed sin, trauma, or addiction that you've been putting off dealing with? It will be a barrier to true joy. One of the reasons it took me so long to complete this book is that God knew I had some big things He wanted me to confess, surrender, and overcome. BIG joy was the trade-off.

4. ***Give it away:*** *"Give thanks to the Lord and proclaim His greatness. Let the whole world know what He has done. Sing to Him; yes, sing His praises. Tell everyone about His wonderful deeds"* (I Chronicles 16:8-9).

One of the best ways to continue to have joy is to give it away. Share what God has revealed to you with others. Talk about His goodness. Testify to His faithfulness. Exalt His name. What's better than having God's amazing gift? Blessing others with it!

I would love to hear about your journey of joy. Please share with me what God has done in your life and how He has blessed you during our time together. Send your story to: nancygarrison@gmail.com.

In His Name,
Nancy

NEXT STOP: Joy

ACKNOWLEDGMENTS

I had no idea when I started this endeavor that it would be such a long, laborious process. I naively believed I could simply write down the thoughts and ideas God gave me and <poof> it would be a devotional book. But God had other plans. He knew that the pruning and blooming along the way would be just as impactful to me (if not more so) than the finished manuscript. All honor and glory to my Creator! Without His perfect patience, guidance, and faithfulness, I would've stayed stuck when it became too difficult.

Mike, you're my biggest cheerleader, regardless of how outrageous my plans or ideas may be. I truly believe if I came to you and said I wanted to build a pirate ship, you would tell me that I'd be the best pirate ever. I love you and appreciate all the ways I get to do life with you.

Kylee Faith and Macey Love, thank you for the endless flow of support and encouragement. You consistently listened to all of my rough drafts, provided thoughtful feedback, and championed me every step of the way. You make life sweeter.

Mom, I love that you were with me on the day that I officially signed my contract to become a published author. Thank you for celebrating with me and for reminding me to trust in the Lord at all times.

NEXT STOP: Joy

Pastor Terrell Huntley, this book wouldn't have happened without you and your leadership. God used you to not only draw me out of my spiral but to lead me down a path where it would point others to Him. Thank you for always being willing to have the hard conversations and for using your gifts to shepherd me.

Gwen Smith, from the moment I met you, you've been coaching someone in my family. I never dreamed it would be me and would involve professional writing. You taught me that the first step was to pray for the women who would be reading my written words. You showed me how to find my "voice" and how to use it to share the message God gave me. You're a gem. You shine brightly in every space you're in.

Thank you to United House Publishing and my personal coach, Elizabeth Hughes, for believing in me and providing an avenue for me to share what God has done in my life.

Thank you to the beautiful bouquet of female friends that God has blessed me with. All of your prayers and cheers, "You got this, girl!" kept me afloat in the days that seemed like I was never going to reach the finish line—a special shout-out to Kathy Boone and Cindy Sacket. You were both uniquely and immensely impactful in my joy journey.

I'm so very grateful that we don't have to travel this adventure alone. God has blessed me with an incredible family, church community, and tribe. I can't wait to see where we get to go next . . .

About the author...
Nancy Garrison is an author, speaker and women's ministry leader based in North Carolina. She enjoys sharing her colorful stories to help women find God's authentic, lasting joy. Nancy is a wife, mother of two adult daughters and grandmother to three mischievous canines.

www.ingramcontent.com/pod-product-compliance
Lightning Source LLC
Chambersburg PA
CBHW070145080526
44586CB00015B/1855